THE FRIENDSHIP STORE

ANDY KIRKPATRICK

EARNSHAW
BOOKS

The Friendship Store

By Andy Kirkpatrick

Trade Paper: 978-988-8843-76-3
Digital: 978-988-8904-01-3

BIOGRAPHY & AUTOBIOGRAPHY

EB217

Published in Hong Kong by Earnshaw Books Ltd.

DEDICATION

In Memory of Lyn and to all those *Liuxuesheng* (international students) who braved China in the 1970s.

Acknowledgments

This book would not have seen the light of day without the wonderful support and encouragement from Graham Earnshaw. Thanks are also due to Victoria Graham for her expert editing. Thanks also to Andrew Molle, Jeremy Mytton, Barclay Thomson and Anto Marden for taking the trouble to read earlier versions of the text and suggesting improvements. Finally, my heartfelt thanks to Adam Williams who believed in the book and thus helped my self-belief.

Contents

THE FRIENDSHIP STORE

1

AN IMPORTANT NATIONWIDE BROADCAST

It was 1976 and we had only been in China since the beginning of
September, nine days, and already the tedium of life at the Beijing
Language Institute was beginning to tell. So we were looking
forward to September 9, as this was to be a holiday, 'Institute
Day'. Why September 9? Because on an earlier September 9,
Chairman Mao Zedong had visited the Institute and done it the
great honor of writing the name of the institute in his calligraphy.
The Chairman's calligraphy had been fixed over the main gate of
the Institute. We all knew about this as every time we walked by
the main gate one of the teachers would ask whether we knew
whose calligraphy it was. After being asked this question several
times it became increasingly difficult not to reply innocently "Lin
Biao?" or "Liu Shaoqi?", earlier colleagues of Mao in the Chinese
Communist Party (CCP) but who had been purged by him (and
in Lin Biao's case, possibly murdered, as the plane in which he
was fleeing China crashed for reasons that have never been fully
explained). There was, inevitably, a huge statue of Mao that
looked down upon us mere mortals as we wandered beneath
his gaze. The statue had not budged during the earthquake that
had razed the city of Tangshan on July 28, killing a quarter of
a million people and causing damage to some buildings at the

Institute, 200 kilometers from the epicenter. But Mao's statue had stood firm.

Preparation of the celebrations for Institute Day were complete. Balloons had been inflated and were hanging in enormous bunches. A stage had been erected on the open ground in front of the residence halls. From the stage, people would be making excruciatingly boring speeches in which they would highlight that great day when 'Our Great Leader Chairman Mao Zedong' had graced the Institute with his presence and that the development of the Institute was being brilliantly guided by the diligent study of the thoughts of Chairman Mao.

But those celebrations were not destined not to take place that September 9, 1976.

On the morning of the ninth we were told there was going to be an 'important nationwide broadcast'. And the balloons came down.

Many of the foreign students had made the most of their day off and had gone into Beijing, planning to return to the Institute for the festivities, scheduled to get underway in the afternoon. As the students started drifting back into the Institute, the speculation about the contents of the broadcast, due to air at 4:00 p.m., increased. It was clearly going to be bad news of some import. Signs that we were to celebrate a special day had been removed. All the decorations, the balloons, the bunting were gone. All that was left was an empty wooden stage.

What was this news? Had there been another natural disaster on the scale of the Tangshan earthquake? Or had a senior member of the Party died? Premier Zhou Enlai had died only in January. Could it possibly be that Mao himself had passed away?

At three in the afternoon, it was all but confirmed that the latter speculation had been accurate. This confirmation was provided by a sudden, painful wail of despair that burst out of the residence hall of the female Chinese students. I had never heard and have since never heard such heart-piercing shrieks of anguish. It was an incredible moment. A group of us had been talking together while waiting outside for the broadcast, speculating about its content, when we were suddenly engulfed by this full-throated cry of despair, as if all hope and joy had been removed from the earth. We were silenced as though our tongues had been frozen by the chill that shuddered through us.

Then the wailing ceased as abruptly as it had begun. The girls emerged from their dormitory and shuffled past us, many still crying and moaning in despair. We later learned they were on their way to a meeting that had been called for Party members. Members of the Communist Party had been given the news an hour before the rest of the nation.

"Well, he's gone then," observed our Newcastle representative, breaking the trancelike silence. Final confirmation that Mao had indeed died was provided at 4:00 p.m.

"Our country, our Party, our army..." began the broadcaster solemnly.

After the broadcast, some of us stood outside on the steps of our hall of residence wondering blindly what Mao's death might hold for the future of China and for our future in China. We were interrupted by the sight of a foreign student from one of the African nations wandering towards us across the grounds. Normally, this would not have been enough for us to stop talking to each other and to stare in open-mouthed amazement at the sight before us. For this fellow did not appear to have been the slightest bit discomfited at the news of Mao's death. He was sporting, and sporting is the word, a multi-colored cotton shirt, and if he wasn't actually snapping his fingers, he was about as close as a man can get to finger-snapping without actually snapping them. His opening words were in keeping with his style, "These Chinese, they are damn quiet folks. What do they do for pleasure around here?"

"Bloody hell, man, don't you know the Chairman's just died?' blurted out our Newcastle representative, incredulously.

No, apparently, he did not. The man had only just arrived in Beijing a couple of days earlier at the start of a four-year course. He spoke not a word of Chinese. He had heard the broadcast—it would have been virtually impossible not to have heard it, given that it was broadcast from every loudspeaker across the nation—but he had not understood a word of it. And had anybody thought to explain what had happened, knowing no Chinese at all, he would have been none the wiser. On learning from us what had happened, the poor man looked mortified at thinking how his behavior must have appeared to the grieving Chinese.

A little later some Chinese began to reappear from their halls. They were all wearing black armbands and white paper chrysanthemums were pinned to their jackets. This signified mourning. On noting this, our quick-thinking leader—each group of foreign students had to appoint a leader through whom the Chinese (in our case a certain Comrade Bi) could relay important information—assumed the responsibility of insuring the group of British students would be appropriately attired. We were dispatched to the nearby village of Five Road Crossroads (*Wu Dao Kou*) with the cloth coupons with which each of us had been assigned on arrival to purchase material, but for clothes rather than for black armbands. With the armbands pinned to our sleeves, but still without the white chrysanthemums, we felt we were suitably attired to set off to pay what turned out to be the first of many sessions of paying last respects to the dead Chairman. One of the classrooms had already been prepared for this purpose, outside of which a queue had formed. We joined the queue, shuffling silently along and entered the room where we were to sign our names in the condolence book. The room was dominated by a large portrait of Mao as it hung from a wall, bordered with black cloth to which white flowers had been pinned around both edges and at the top and bottom of the frame.

We went forward to stand respectfully with heads bowed before this portrait to the strains of sombre funereal music. We then filed out of the room, shaking hands with the line-up of teachers and cadres, all of whom were weeping noisily and copiously.

The following days were taken up with memorial services of one sort or another, while the radio and loudspeakers continued to broadcast, on the hour every hour, the announcement of Mao's death. These hourly announcements were followed by solemn music, including a slow moving and mournful version of the "Internationale". As a result, that inspiring call to revolution today inspires in me only thoughts of solemnity and death.

Among all the memorial services was the Institute's formal memorial. For this, we had to learn how to make, not only chrysanthemums out of white crinkly paper, but also large paper wreaths. I had not expected to learn these skills and I have to confess that I never got beyond the paper flower stage. Even then my flowers never looked quite right, as I'm 'all fingers and thumbs' when it comes to delicate wrapping. Family members have never had to read the accompanying card to know who their present came from. The only item I managed to construct during woodworking classes was a small rectangular wooden box that sort of lurched to one side and in which my darling mother kept pens and pencils until her dying day.

To the completed wreaths – fortunately there were handicraft wizards within the group – we attached two thickish strips of white ribbon, upon the first of which was written "The Foreign

Students at Beijing Language Institute". Upon the second was written what translates rather prosaically as "May the Great Leader and Teacher Mao Zedong Never Rot." Wreaths were placed both inside and within the main hall where the official tribute was to take place.

During the official memorial, the hall was a mass of white wreaths, all of which were covered with white paper chrysanthemums. But instead of filing solemnly past the portrait of the Chairman as we had done on previous occasions, this time many members of the Institute's hierarchy made speeches. Listening to these speeches was excruciatingly painful. And it was also embarrassing. The speakers all found it difficult to mention Mao's name without breaking down. One poor teacher hardly managed to complete her eulogy, wailing at her own mention of Mao's name while tears streamed from her raw red eyes and down her pallid cheeks. The embarrassing, if not to say distasteful to some of us, part of all this was that it seemed as if much of this weeping and wailing was an act, a performance in which people were expected to put on to a show grief. Professional mourners are a Chinese cultural tradition.

These memorial services at the Institute turned out to be mere preliminaries to the main event, the Lying-in-State. We had been informed on the Sunday that we had been afforded the great honor of being invited to go to the Great Hall of the People to pay our last respects before the Chairman's corpse itself. The rest of Sunday was taken up with a frenzy of white flower-making.

Monday, on the day we had attended the Lying in State, a multi-racial bunch of foreign students congregated in front of the Slogan Tower that served as the Institute's focal point. All were dressed in the equivalent of their Sunday best, with black armbands and white paper flower accessories. We were waiting for the buses that were to take us to Tian An Men Square and the

Great Hall of the People where Mao was lying in state. A fleet of long green single-decker buses began to arrive. These too had been made-up for the occasion, as each had large white paper flowers attached to their radiator, giving them the appearance of having somehow sprouted white noses. We clambered aboard the buses to which we had been assigned and the procession started to wend its way slowly through the main gate on its way to the Great Hall.

The streets seemed only slightly less crowded than usual, but black armbands were everywhere and the ubiquitous and identical portraits of Mao that had only a day or two earlier being wishing the Chairman a long life were all now bordered in black. Ubiquitous slogans urged the people to turn 'grief into strength'.

Emerging from the streets that zig-zag haphazardly around Beijing into the vast width of the city's main boulevard and Tian An Men Square was like moving from a vibrant jostling city to a silent forbidding State. This part of Beijing is home to a series of ugly edifices in the style of what might be called May Day architecture. Lowering buildings, Orwellian specters and the huge square itself, which created images of military might accompanied by the sounds of battalions of army boots smacking against the stone paving flags. The Chinese gates on either side of this open square look bizarrely out of place as they led onto this massive square.

The buses drew up outside the Great Hall. We disembarked and took our place in the queue that was moving slowly, step by step, as though in time with the funeral dirges that were playing, on towards the monstrous doors of the Great Hall. Officials were on hand to ensure that all mourners were wearing their black armbands.

Eventually we entered the Great Hall itself and the sudden immersion into air-conditioning sent shivers down the line. Before entering the actual room where Mao's body lay, we shook hands with senior Communist Party members who were arraigned in a row leading up to the entrance to the room. One such was Chen Yonggui, a towel-turbaned peasant from Shanxi Province, who had been promoted to the dizzying heights of the Politburo for his success in making his village, *Da Zhai*, a model commune. Peasants from other agricultural communes were all encouraged to learn and sing that popular ditty, "Peasants learn from Da Zhai." I braced myself for a knuckle-crunching handshake from this man with his weather-beaten face that spelled the hardship of many years spent outdoors, but was offered a lifeless limp hand, no doubt the consequence of a thousand handshakes.

After the handshaking, we moved forward to take our places at the foot of the glass casket in which the body lay. Behind the casket stood a gallery of ornate wreaths. But, at the foot of the casket lay Mao's wife, Jiang Qing's wreath, which, in an uncharacteristic but clearly contrived show of modesty, was signed simply, "Your student". This wreath, along with the others laid by the other members of what became known as the Gang of Four and who were later blamed for Mao's disastrous excesses, was cut from the official film of the Lying in State. When, some months later, I pointed this omission out to my Chinese roommates in Shanghai, I was told this was not a distortion of history at all because the film was not a historical document.

As we stood in lines four-deep at the foot of the casket, we became aware of members of the People's Liberation Army lining either side of it. Presumably these were members of Mao's private bodyguard, now protecting him even in death.

The body itself was not an attractive sight. A waxen image with cheeks puffed up by some injected chemical or other to make the corpse appear healthier than the living version. But, I suppose this is the task of most undertakers. The skin had assumed a murky combination of dark yellow and gray.(1)

We stood at the foot of the casket for exactly three minutes, three minutes that seemed a lot longer than that, before proceeding past the right side of the casket, back through the cold shadows of the Hall and out into the brilliant September sunshine.

Those of us who thought that our visit to the Lying-in-State would mark the culmination of funeral broadcasts, funereal music and tears of confected grief had not taken into account the Chinese stamina for such matters. However, even those who understood the importance the Chinese attach to periods of formal mourning were staggered to discover on going to class on Tuesday morning that the funeral broadcast was to be used as teaching material. And in two forms: a tape of the broadcast was used for listening comprehension, and a transcript for reading comprehension.

The classes were grotesque. The teachers sobbed unceasingly through the classes. The students, initially stunned and embarrassed, then became angry with the teachers who, far from 'turning grief into strength' were positively wallowing in it. The tape was played over and over again. The transcript was read over and over again. We were given paragraphs of the transcript to memorize for homework (never done). It was a week before classes returned to anything approaching normal.

But what would count as normal? How would Mao's death affect the lives of the Chinese? This was the man who had led the CCP to victory in the civil war against Chiang Kai-shek in 1949. He had since then ruled over China as a demi-god. When he feared his rule was being threatened in the mid-1960s, he unleashed the Cultural Revolution to trash, and in many cases exterminate, his enemies, along with millions of innocent victims. With his death, what would now befall the nation? Who would seize power? I had often wondered what might happen in the event of Mao's death, but I was not expecting him to die only nine days after we arrived. I would now be in a position to see how China might change and what those changes might mean for the Chinese. But I had no such thoughts on arrival for my first day of a four-year degree in Chinese at Leeds University.

2

INTRODUCTION TO CHINESE

"It's very hard work, you won't be able to spend much time partying and you'll find it hard to get a job at the end of it. And, as you have been told, you have to do a double degree—your choice is one of history, geography, economics or politics—and do final papers in that as well. It will take at least four years of hard full-time study. So if anyone of you wants to reconsider enrolling in the Chinese Department, please feel free to leave the room."

This was the rather less than encouraging opening salvo of the Deputy Head of the Chinese Department at Leeds University as he addressed the eighteen assembled first-year students on the opening day of the term. After his opening salvo, sixteen of us remained. It was 1968 and I was one of the sixteen.

Rather than being economical with the truth, the Deputy Head had been effusive with it. It had, indeed, been hard work. I still hear Mr Li's plaintive call in his class of conversational Chinese.

"When we learn language, we make many mistake. We must struggle together."

I am still astounded to remember that I willingly spent many hours in the Brotherton Library, happily practicing writing

Chinese characters while my peers were carousing in the local pubs. Luckily, the Brotherton closed at 10:00 p.m. in those days, allowing enough time for the studious to down a couple of pints before closing time. My favorite haunt was the Fenton, a short walk down the hill from the library, a walk considerably enhanced by the self-satisfaction of hours spent in the library coupled with the expectation of the first pint of the deliciously creamy Tetley's bitter .

Yes, it had been hard work, and far from taking four years to complete, I finally graduated in 1976, some eight years after enrolling. My delay in graduating was caused by my 'dropping out' and spending a couple of years in Europe and Taiwan and then being allowed to re-enter the third year of the Leeds degree by an extraordinarily understanding head of department.

Fast forward to 1976 and I, with my wife, Lyn, newly minted graduates of Chinese studies, were part of the group of fifteen British students with degrees in Chinese who had been selected for British Council scholarships to spend a year as postgraduate students of Chinese in Chinese universities. Ethnically Chinese, Lyn had been born in Guyana and raised in London and had studied Chinese at Leeds. The others came from Cambridge, Edinburgh, London and Oxford universities. We congregated in Hong Kong, nervously awaiting our trip across the border. We were nervous as, in those days, the border between Hong Kong and China was virtually closed. One took the train from Hong Kong to the border post at Lo Wu. One then disembarked and walked into China across the alarmingly rickety Lo Wu Bridge from where we got a Chinese train to Beijing. And although those travelers who had made this trip would wax lyrical about the romance of having to walk into China, my feelings as we stumbled across the bridge were some distance from romantic.

I was conscious of entering a closed country about which little was known. The stress of the occasion had an unfortunate effect on my bowels and I was becoming desperate, struggling with my luggage, to cross the bridge and reach the Chinese border station of Shenzhen and find a loo. My first glimpse of a Chinese person in China was, perhaps appropriately enough, of a member of the fearsome People's Liberation Army, or PLA. He appeared to be wearing a made-to-measure-somebody-else's uniform, topped off with the famous green cap with the red star in the middle. On his feet he wore a pair of what looked surprisingly like slippers made out of black cloth. He was standing at rigid attention with a rifle on his shoulder, chin-up, chest-out, and eyes-front. And he looked about thirteen years old. I gave him a nervous smile as I stumbled past him.

As I was to discover, public toilets in Chinese were generally to be avoided at all costs. I was lucky, therefore, that my first experience of one was clean and I was able to rejoin the others, feeling far more at ease than I had been a few minutes earlier.

The next encounter with Chinese was with the customs officials. Having had some unhappy experiences with customs officials in my time, viewing some as a form of uniformed thieves, I was relieved and pleasantly surprised to find that these fellows were smilingly polite and courteous. Customs formalities over, we were shepherded into the waiting room of Shenzhen station. Today it serves a population of thirteen million and is a vast railway hub with long distance high-speed trains connecting China; a small metro runs beneath it. In 1976 it was a two-platform hick station serving an insignificant village.

We had two hours to wait for our train to Beijing. This gave us the first real opportunity we had had to observe each other. Here we were, fourteen strangers (the fifteenth member would join us in Beijing) sitting in a bleak station waiting room in a setting culturally, politically and geographically far removed from our comfort zones. I imagined Agatha Christie, if she were able to observe the scene, gleefully feeling this would provide excellent potential.

There was apprehension in the air. People glanced surreptitiously at each other hoping that their glances would not be noticed. Some attempted an air of distanced nonchalance. One, a girl clearly a devotee of the Stephen Potter School of one-upmanship, produced a Chinese novel, while making a show when turning a page. A boy, wearing a Che Guevara-type beret, lounged, perhaps attempting to look the revolutionary. Then, a strange thing happened. One of the group took out his wallet and began to carefully go through the notes within it. He took each note out, turned it over as if to examine it minutely, replaced it and then repeated the procedure with the next note and so on. He also placed his coins under the same close scrutiny. And then other members of the group started to do the same thing, presenting a startling variation of the looking-at-the-ceiling theme. Rather than being genuinely interested in the Chinese currency — although it was not completely without interest — it was something to be pretending to be doing like reading a paper upside down as one does, for example, when waiting for test results in the GP's surgery or when the pilot has just announced over the tannoy that the landing gear isn't working.

No doubt the Chinese bystanders attributed this scrutiny of notes and coins to some form of capitalist reflex. At the same time, they would have been taken aback at the amount of money on show. We had each changed ten British pounds into Chinese currency, and each therefore had the equivalent of an average monthly Chinese salary in our pockets.

Then, lunch was served. The food was simple but excellent — a variety of fresh vegetables, rice and soup; and there was plenty of Chinese beer. The atmosphere warmed and we started to talk to each other.

The first part of the train journey, from Shenzhen to Canton, was one of air-conditioned comfort. Tea was served by 'girl comrades' wearing extremely baggy trousers and rather fetching tunic tops. Throughout the journey we were treated to political propaganda delivered over the loudspeakers in shrill, almost hysterical, tones informing us of the Chairman's views on a range of subjects. I wondered whether I would ever get used to this method of propaganda being piped and pumped almost constantly through loudspeakers, even in open air spaces. No, is the answer.

We arrived in Canton, tired, dirty and in much need of both bath and bed. Our welcoming committee had other plans.

The China Travel Service (CTS) was at that time a heartless organization whose main aim appeared to be to extract as much foreign currency as possible from foreign tourists while preventing them from seeing much of China. Only those parts of China that *must* be seen are on any itinerary. Members from the China Travel Service were waiting dutifully for us at the station. And as we were due to leave for Beijing that evening, they had decided we must see as many of the 'must-sees' as possible in the time available. A bus had been laid on for us – at great expense, we were later to discover – and we spent the late afternoon and early evening being whisked around those place the CTS had determined would be seen. First, the Martyrs' Park. The main point of this visit was to be told the history behind the Martyrs' Memorial, which commemorates the death of several thousand members of the nascent Chinese Communist Party in what became known as the Guangzhou Uprising, a failed attempt to overthrow the government led by Chiang Kai-shek in 1927. This, of course, is a key event in the history of the CCP and it would have been interesting to have been able to learn more about the uprising, but our guide was more intent on informing us that the calligraphy engraved on the monument was that of Zhou Enlai, the recently deceased Foreign Minister and who had been, for many years, Mao's right-hand man. Then, zipping past beds abloom with beautiful flowers, it was off to the Porcelain Museum. I was expecting to see examples of delicate pieces from China's history, a Tang plate or vase or two, but what we were shown were truly hideous sculptures of heroic and idealized figures of the socialist revolution, depicted striving forward, muscles rippling and eyes gleaming with the righteousness of the indoctrinated. Idols of clay, indeed.

Next, it was time to rush for dinner. This was to be a banquet but not one on which we were consulted about what we might want to eat or where we might want to eat it, but how much we wanted to spend on it. We were offered a range of four possible prices ranging from ludicrously expensive to only absurdly so. We chose the cheapest of the four options, a choice that was not received with equanimity on the part of our hosts. I suspect that they would have received a cut and the size of the cut depended upon the expense of the banquet ordered. Anyway, we found ourselves at the North Garden Restaurant.

Despite serving the 'cheapest' banquet, the North Garden Restaurant was not a restaurant for the average Chinese diner, but one that catered exclusively for foreigners and Overseas Chinese visitors. It comprised several separate dining rooms attractively 'necklaced' around a small indoor pond over which several hump-backed stone bridges crossed. We were ushered into one of the private dining rooms, feeling somewhat self-conscious and out of place and, in my case, not at all hungry. I suspect what we all wanted most was a shower and a comfortable bed.

The meal took an unusual course, but given our state of

minds, possibly a predictable one. Unsmiling waitresses arrived in alarming frequency carrying dish after dish to us diners, most of whom wanted to be somewhere else. However, the more the dishes that arrived, the fewer the diners there were to eat them. The strain of the day had begun to tell. First, one of our number felt sick and had to leave the table, accompanied by a chaperone-comforter. Then another was sick and went off with another comforter. By the time the soup, traditionally the final dish of a Chinese banquet, was served, only eight of the fourteen who had sat down to dinner remained at the table. But, there was not time to drink the soup, as the CTS chivvied us out of the restaurant to rush us off to the station to catch the Beijing train. Before boarding the train, the charming CTS cadres demanded payment for the banquet. We breathed a collective sigh of relief that we had opted for the cheapest banquet on offer.

3

To Beijing

The train journey from Guangzhou to Beijing took about thirty hours. As someone else (The British Council? The British Embassy? — whoever it was, thank you) had paid for the train tickets we traveled first class. In those days there were three classes on Chinese trains, namely 'soft-sleeping', 'soft-sitting' and 'hard sitting'. 'Soft-sleeping' class entitled us to the comparative luxury of a four berth couchette. My wife and I found ourselves sharing with two Chinese whom those who say they can't tell Chinese people apart should meet. One was a paunchy, comfortable man with a weather-beaten face contoured with purple veins that suggested a man who enjoyed his cups. The other was a type of whom Caesar was always being told to beware, a thin, hungry and twitchy character whose expression of exquisite discomfort and the awkward angle at which he sat advertised the possibility of a chronic haemorrhoidal complaint.

The comfortable fellow was an officer in the PLA. The PLA uniform did not have any military markings of rank, but judging from the number of buttons and pockets on his green tunic, he was a senior officer. Added to his age — he appeared to be about 60 — and the fact that he was traveling first class meant we were sharing a couchette with a man of some distinction. He was also a jovial and chatty chap who showed great interest in both us and in England, plying us with questions, with a particular focus on the doings of the Royal Family. He was less forthcoming about his own background and job, however, about which he remained silent.

"Are you a member of the People's Liberation Army?" I asked.

"I can't say," he replied.

But he at least was happy to talk to us about us. In sharp contrast, 'yonder Cassius' had no small talk or any talk at all. His only utterance to us throughout the entire journey was when I asked him what he did for a living. The first time I asked him this question, he either didn't hear or pretended not to, as he continued to gaze out of the window with the pained expression of one who disapproved of everything his eyes fell upon, whether it be paddy fields with water buffalo or mountains and rivers, what the Chinese call 'mountain-water' scenery. To attract his attention, I gently touched the sleeve of his gray, well-tailored Mao jacket and repeated my question.

"What do you do?"

I can't say," he replied. Angrily flicking my hand from his sleeve, he turned his face to stare at me with complete Obadiah Slopian disdain and announced through his thin lips,

"I'm a proletarian."

This of course was a good thing to be in the China of the time. But it was also the case that no real member of the proletariat could afford to be traveling first class. And the cut of his Mao jacket suggested a high-level CCP functionary.

We spent two nights on the train. Two extremely hot nights. Lyn and I had been assigned to the two bunks on one side of the couchette, the general and the proletarian the two on the other side. A tussle ensued between the two of them. The general wanted the window open; the proletarian wanted the fan on. The general, who was in the top bunk, did not want the fan on because it was perilously close to his head. The proletarian on the lower bunk did not want the window open as we were being pulled by a steam engine and he did not relish the prospect of being slowly buried in his sleep by the smut and soot being emitted from the engine. The result was a 0-0 draw. The window remained closed and the fan off.

A joy of traveling by train in China — and there weren't many — was the presence of a dining car. The food was excellent, usually some form of stir fried pork or chicken and fresh leafy greens with steamed rice. We were only later to discover what a luxury it was to get meat and a variety of vegetables. The food was also very cheap. After many years traveling and eating all over China I developed a basic rule of thumb. The cheaper the food, the better it is. Simple 'home' cooking beats a banquet any day. And a real treat was that bottled beer was also available. Chinese beer is good and owes much to European brewing techniques. Tsingtao (Qing Dao) is probably the most famous today and was originally brewed by Germans in their concession in Qing Dao (hence the name) in Shandong Province. Many years later, when travel around China had become less restricted, I spent a few days in Qing Dao and tried to persuade, unsuccessfully as it turned out, the guards on the gates of the Qing Dao brewery to let me in and have a look around.

The only drawback about the beer on the train was that the bottles were not chilled, but kept in crates in the pantry. I asked the waiter whether it would be possible to put a bottle or two in the pantry fridge for me, something he was only too happy to do. I was then able to indulge in the most simple but greatest of pleasures — sipping cold beer on the train to Beijing while watching the Chinese countryside slide past.

Our train finally pulled into Beijing railway station at 9:00 a.m. in the morning. As we clambered down onto the platform, wrestling with luggage and no doubt looking somewhat bedraggled after our journey, a young, slim, almost waif-like and slightly dishevelled-looking chap, wearing blue jeans and an open-neck shirt came tripping along the platform.

"Are you the British students?" he asked while, with his open palm, brushing back the black hair that fell anarchically over his forehead.

"Yes," one of us replied.

"Good, then follow me."

Off we traipsed after him like faithful dogs keeping to heel. Down, through and up out of an underpass we trudged. And then I broke ranks to go in search of a loo. I mentioned earlier that there were not many pleasures to be had when traveling by train in China and visiting the toilets was not one of them. They were all squat toilets and most were simply disgustingly filthy with a gag-making smell of excrement and urine. They were thus to be avoided except in cases of dire need. I had avoided them for as long as I felt I could but about fifteen minutes before the train was due to arrive in Beijing, the time had come. It was when arriving at the toilet that I discovered the Chinese custom of locking all toilets half an hour before trains are due to arrive at main stations. Hence my need for a toilet at Beijing Railway station and delight at finding one. This delight was heightened by the realization that, as I was not sure how to ask where a loo was in vernacular Chinese, I was doubly relieved to see the sign indicating the gents. I virtually skipped towards it but have to confess to a slight lessening of stride as I entered the toilets and absorbed the scene before me and as my shoes absorbed the liquid around them. For, before me, were two rows of open squat-type toilets all of which were occupied by squatting Chinese doing their business, most of whom were reading newspapers — shortly to be put to other use — and smoking. I then made the mistake of looking down and found my shoes standing in a pool of liquid lapping against the sides. The composition of the liquid was uncertain but certainly not one to investigate. It's funny how what, only a few seconds earlier, seemed essential can suddenly seem less important. I convinced myself I would be able to wait a little longer. I re-joined the others and the queue to register, officially, our arrival in Beijing. The man from the embassy hovered protectively while we had our travel passes stamped by a stern-looking individual wearing a white uniform and a smart blue hat. His right arm went up, down, stamp, up, down stamp, up down stamp. We were all soon in possession of stamped passes bearing official bureaucratic recognition that we had arrived in Beijing.

Once assured we had all received our stamps, the man from the Embassy left us to return to a world of move and counter-move that he had interrupted to join us — he had a tennis match to complete. His parting words were, "Dinner tonight". His departure left us in what we were to discover were the somewhat less than capable hands of the cadre from the Foreign Languages Institute, one Comrade Bi.

4

COMRADE BI

Comrade Bi was a man of small stature who wore a pair of extraordinarily unflattering spectacles. This, of course, would not be enough to make him stand out in a typical Chinese crowd. When not smiling, he appeared stern and serious. But when smiling — and this was frequently as he often smiled to cover his embarrassment and he was often embarrassed — he was hard not to notice. This was because of his teeth, only assumed to exist when his face was at rest, announced themselves as it were with a drum roll. As soon as he smiled, his teeth took over. His lips appeared to disappear, his nose, of no great moment in the first place, seemed to vanish as his teeth took over the stage. His eyes wrinkled to thin strips. When smiling, Comrade Bi simply became a set of teeth, between which nervous giggles somehow managed to prise their way.

The smile also appeared when Comrade Bi was nervous and, if any man had a right to be nervous, it was Comrade Bi. He had been appointed to be the cadre in charge of foreign students at the Beijing Foreign Language Institute when it re-opened its doors to them in 1973. It was not an easy or enviable job. His main responsibility was to deny requests made by foreign students while seeming not to deny them their requests. He had mastered the first part of the job, but his technique was still rusty when it came to the second part. Lyn and I were soon to encounter personal experience of this. On discovering that there were apparently no married quarters available for students at the Institute, we politely asked Comrade Bi whether it might not be possible for us to cohabit, as we knew that married students had been able to share rooms in earlier years.

"Comrade Bi," I ventured, "you know Lyn and I are married and we would therefore like to be able to share a room together."

Comrade Bi's face became all smile and teeth, but he replied, "I'm very sorry and I'm afraid to tell you that there are no married quarters here."

"But we know married students have shared rooms here in the past," we argued.

Comrade Bi (smile/teeth) replied, "I'm so sorry but there is now a new regulation."

"What regulation?"

Comrade BI (smile/teeth) replied again, "I am so sorry but here is a new regulation."

"Would Comrade Bi please ask the authorities to let us have a look at this new regulation?"

Smile/teeth/giggle, "I will try."

The giggle clearly meant there was no chance at all that the authorities would ever let us see such a regulation, not least because such a regulation did not exist. Nevertheless, we kept at him for a couple of weeks but all we ever received were smiles, displays of teeth and nervous giggles. We never got our married quarters, either at the Institute, nor later when we moved to Shanghai, to Fudan University.

5

SETTLING IN: BOOZE, A PUNCH,
AN EARTHQUAKE AND THE SUMMER PALACE

The Beijing Foreign Languages Institute (later to become the University of Language and Culture) is in the northwest suburbs of Beijing (and what was then countryside) and tucked between two small villages called *Wu Dao Kou* (Five Road Crossroads) and *Si Dao Kou* (Four Road Crossroads). As befits its name, *Wu Dao Kou* was the bigger of the two villages, and the livelier. There was an indoor market where a range of goods from bicycles and heavy winter coats to electrical appliances and stamps were sold. There was a photographic studio, a book shop, a number of small food stores, a bicycle repair workshop, a supermarket and a working man's club. There were also two restaurants, one Muslim-run, the other a very down-to-earth basic Chinese restaurant. No frills. The latter was very popular with students from the Institute, and for many it was the first restaurant they tried in China.

The restaurant itself was divided into three parts. The main entrance opened into a snack bar, which was invariably packed with locals slurping large bowls of noodles. The snack bar also housed the beer and alcohol counter. The beer was 'draft' in that it arrived piped up from metal barrels through rubber hoses to be poured into large plastic jugs. Beer and a highly potent concoction sold under the catch-all label of '*baijiu*' or white spirit, were the most popular drinks and consumed in quantity by the 'masses'. There are upmarket and very expensive versions of '*baijiu*', the best known of which is *Mao Tai* which is AA.

On my first visit to the restaurant, I was astonished to see so many flushed faces. Many Chinese find it hard to conceal that they have been drinking as their faces soon take on a rich red hue. That I was surprised by what was an extremely common sight underlined how little I knew about the day-to-day lives of the Chinese. My initial surprise was soon replaced with a feeling of reassurance. Enjoying a beer or two is a commonly shared international pleasure. Somehow, seeing all these chaps with their flushed faces laughing with each other as they downed their beer suddenly made the prospect of spending the next year or so in China a much less intimidating prospect than it had been. I thought to myself, "I can happily communicate with fellow beer drinkers." Little did I realize how difficult it would be to share a drink of any sort with the local population.

The large room behind the snack bar section of the restaurant housed the main dining area. Off this were a small number of screened-off areas where private parties could be catered for. Each of these contained a circular table, large enough to seat ten diners around it. It was in one such a setting that an incident took place that entered the folk lore of the foreign students at the Language Institute. A group of foreign students, all from countries that were classified as belonging to the 'third world', had enjoyed a meal during which several jugs of beer had been consumed. All was well until the bill arrived. The size of the bill caused a stir with the students feeling they had been vastly overcharged and expressed disbelief that they could possibly have consumed as many jugs of beer as noted on the flimsy piece of paper that was the bill. The patron assured the students that the bill was correct. The students were not convinced. Heated exchanges then took place between the students, the patron and several of the waiters. The students then left the restaurant without paying. On the short walk back to the Institute they were approached by a policeman. He had been called by the patron of the restaurant who had explained to him what had happened and then tasked him with the onerous duty of getting the students to pay their bill. The policeman approached the students and addressed them as Chinese were all advised to address foreigners.

"Foreign friends," he said, "you have not paid this bill, please pay."

The next thing the poor man knew was that he was flat on his back in the middle of the road, having been floored by an irate student's punch. That punch led to repercussions. The relevant Embassy was informed, the student hauled before his Ambassador and then put on a plane home.

The repatriation led, in turn, to further repercussions, especially for those students who came from those countries that comprised the so-called third world. The term originally referred to those countries that were not aligned with either side during the Cold War, the two sides being NATO, the Western bloc and the other being the communist bloc. But the term was also used to refer to the 'developing' countries of Africa, Asia and Latin America. The United States and countries which seemed to be aligned with it (The United Kingdom and Australia, for example) constituted the first world and the communist bloc, the second world. However, the Chinese shifted the meanings. In 1970s China, the US was the only first world country. Western European nations were considered the second world and the developing countries the third world.

The students who had been invited to China came from

either the second world or the third world. At the time there were no American students in China. But the students from the second world (such as the fifteen British students) and those from the third world were in China for very different reasons and under very different circumstances. The second world students were all graduates of Chinese from universities in their respective countries and had voluntarily applied to come to China to further their studies of Chinese. We all had some four years of studying Chinese under our belts and, to a certain level, could read and write the language. In stark contrast, the students from the third world, who, unlike the second world students, were all males, had often been 'volunteered' by their governments to take up scholarships offered by the Chinese in subjects associated with nation-building of some sort. These subjects included, for example, textile manufacturing and a range of disciplines in engineering. The second world students all had some Chinese and were in China to pursue postgraduate studies in some aspect of Chinese culture (literature or history, for example). The third world students had no Chinese and were in China to pursue four or five- undergraduate programmes in technical subjects. They all had to spend *at least* the first year of their stay in China studying Chinese at the Institute before being allowed to commence their studies proper. There were few genuine volunteers among this group. Typically, applications in response to advertized scholarships to study in China did not flood in. As a result, governments nominated those who would take up the scholarships. One such student was the son of his country's ambassador to China and who happened to be staying with him in Beijing. When the country in question received only three applications for the five scholarships on offer, the Ambassador promptly enrolled his son in the programme. One came to feel sorry for this poor chap — although poor he was not, but a member of his country's elite who wore exquisitely tailored clothes, smoked Dunhill cigarettes, which he flamboyantly lit with a gold lighter. He proved to be less than an ideal student. More of him later.

Basically, therefore, the great majority of the third world students were in China involuntarily, had no intrinsic interest in China or its culture and were very unhappy to be there. When the third world students got letters from friends who had been posted elsewhere, their sense of having drawn the short straw increased greatly. For example, letters from fellow students who had been sent to Patrice Lumumba University in Moscow typically reported the grand time they were having in Moscow with plenty of parties, plenty to drink and plenty of girls to drink and party with. Such news caused the mood of their Beijing compatriots to sink even further. Girls and parties to go to were in short supply in the Beijing of the 1970s.

So, to return to the repercussions to the repatriation of the third world student who had clocked a member of the Chinese police force: most third world students were very unhappy at being in China and getting sent home was what most prayed for. Then, one of their number demonstrated how easily this could be achieved. Simply thump a Chinese policeman. One has to feel a certain sympathy for the poor Chinese cop who was the subject of the second attempt to prove the theory. Like many of his counterparts, he would have learned from reading countless articles in his copy of the People's Daily newspaper about how the Chinese were 'great friends' with the peoples of the third world. But then one such great friend tried to punch him. The respective embassies saw through the scheme and swiftly and urgently put an end to this method of repatriation, so policeman punching came to an end. Yet a driver from one of the third world embassies discovered an alternative pathway to immediate repatriation. He exposed himself to a Chinese sales girl in a local department store. He was on the first plane home.

The theme of friendship between the Chinese and the peoples of the world was pervasive in the propaganda, but seldom realized, in fact. An example were the stores called The Friendship Stores. These stores were state-run operations and were opened in the 1950s to cater to Soviet and other experts who were living in China. They sold items unobtainable in 'normal' Chinese stores (where very little of anything was actually obtainable), including chocolates, Western newspapers, a wide range of alcohol, both Chinese and foreign, as well as high-quality Chinese handicrafts and clothes. The stores were out of bounds to the great majority of Chinese — high-level cadres were able to use them — and goods, for some years in the 1980s, could only be purchased with foreign currency certificates. At the time I was in China, the stores accepted the Chinese currency, *renminbi* (people's dollars). Despite their name, the stores were anything but friendly, hence, the title of this book. Bored attendants were well-practiced at avoiding a customer's eye. Catching a French waiter's attention was a breeze by comparison. On occasion, a sales assistant would have to be awakened from slumber. After feeling a sense of triumph on finally catching a sales' assistant attention and asking for a particular item, triumph would be followed by deflation as the sales assistant murmured the phrase which came to be dreaded by many customers. '*Meiyou-le*' (have none), the sales assistant would mutter, often without making any attempt to see if the item was in stock or not. I had the not infrequent experience of pointing to the very item requested on a shelf behind the assistant after she had '*meiyou-le-d*' me. This was never received with a smiling, "Oh I'm sorry, here you are." Instead, a serious case of the sulks would descend upon the sales assistant, as she then painstakingly filled out the sales coupon (this required several copies and this, in turn, required several pieces of flimsy and fiddly carbon paper to be inserted between the pages of the sales booklet). The customer then had to take the appropriate copy to the cash clerk whose 'station' was separate and often some distance away. One then presented the required money or coupons, whereupon the cash clerk would stamp the docket, which the customer then took back to the original sales assistant to collect the item in question. If only buying a single item, significant time had to be invested in the trip to the Friendship Store. Anyone wanting to buy several items from different parts of the store was advised to take rations and reading matter to see them through.

Even so, a trip to the Friendship Store helped add a smidgen of excitement to life at the Language Institute. The Institute was a bleak place with a certain prison-like aura about it. Drab concrete blocks housed both classrooms and halls of residence. These were surrounded by a high brick wall, breached only by a North Gate and a South Gate. The gates were locked at midnight. Having been to a British public school, I probably adapted better to the environment than most.

To add to the general air of desolation, a series of ugly makeshift earthquake shelters had been constructed throughout the grounds, looking like so many giant worm casts. These had been built in the wake of the terrifyingly destructive 1976 earthquake which devastated the city of Tangshan, costing a quarter of a million lives. Beijing also suffered some damage. Fortunately, the earthquake had done little damage to the Institute. A few cracks had appeared in some classroom blocks and the top floor of one of the halls of residence had been cleared as the chimney on that block had been breached. The Institute reported no casualties, other than that of an Ethiopian student. When the earthquake hit in the early hours of the morning, he woke, dashed to the window of his room on the top (fourth) floor of his hall of residence and duly leaped from it in a daring attempt to seek succor in the branches of a neighboring tree. Whether the tree would have been able to provide the succor he was so eagerly seeking will never be known: he missed it. By the grace of his God, he only suffered two broken ankles. His was the only physical injury recorded. The dignity of the eyebrow-raising number of male Chinese students who emerged, in varying states of undress, from the girls' hall of residence may well have suffered. History does not relate what punishment they received for their nocturnal adventures, but the story certainly made the Chinese students seem far more human to us, than the sexless comrades their dress and behavior suggested.

The Tangshan Earthquake also interrupted the night of the quondam Prime Minister of Australia, Gough Whitlam and his wife, Margaret. They were on a tour of China they were unlikely to forget. Both Whitlams come in the family-economy size and were in bed in Tianjin when the earthquake struck. The famous Australian cartoonist, Peter Nicholson, drew a cartoon which portrayed the Whitlams in some disarray in bed with the caption, "Did the earth move for you too, Dear?' That the Whitlams bought the cartoon and hung it above their bed is compelling evidence that they had a sense of humor.

The bleak atmosphere not only surrounded the grounds and the buildings of the Institute, but seeped through the walls of those buildings, along the ill-lit corridors and into the small rooms themselves. Each room was furnished with two beds, two tables, two wardrobes, two chairs and a radiator. Despite their uninviting similarity to cells, they developed individual characters as they took on or reflected the idiosyncrasies of their inmates.

A prime example of such idiosyncrasy, if not utter idiocy, was provided by the room of a West German student. He decided that he would place his bed on top of the two wardrobes so that it spanned them like a bridge. To get into bed, he had to clamber up on to the table and then lever himself up into it. He decided to place his bed atop the wardrobes for two reasons. The first being, he argued, that it would provide more space. This, to be fair, it did. The second reason he put forward for placing his bed on top of the wardrobes was that it would give him early warning of any future aftershock or earthquake. Again, it was hard to argue against this logic, but one got the feeling one was in the presence of someone who was seriously unhinged.

In early September and having had a few of days to settle in, we were escorted on our first 'sight-seeing' tour. This was to the Summer Palace. We were chaperoned by several teachers and cadres, whose roles were never fully clear, and the ever-present Comrade Bi. We were also accompanied by some Chinese students who were studying 'foreign' languages at the Institute, mostly English. We must have made a curious spectacle, for we were clearly two quite separate groups of students. One group comprised what must have looked like an anarchic bunch of disheveled students, some males with long hair, others with beards, females with painted fingernails and some wearing perfume. The second group comprised a tightly disciplined cohort of males with closely cropped hair all wearing identical Mao trouser suits, and of females all with plaited hair and all wearing identical Mao trouser suits. Some girls daringly allowed a splash of color to show pushing up out of the neck of their Mao jackets. We later learned that they were not wearing blouses as it might appear, but simply had a strip of colored cloth tied around their necks.

Although these groups of foreign and Chinese students might

have been expected to take the opportunity to mingle on such occasions as this trip to the Summer Palace, it was in fact virtually impossible for members of one group to get to know members of the other. This sad fact had nothing to do with the Chinese and foreign students themselves, who would have welcomed the opportunity to get to know and learn something about each other. The cause lay in the restrictions placed on foreign students by the Chinese authorities – represented by Comrade Bi and his ilk – coupled with the fear the Chinese students had of being seen to communicate with foreigners, for which they would be criticized and have to undergo forms of self-criticism. Although the official Chinese bureaucratic term for foreign students is 'foreign friends', it was a rare occasion when a foreign student was even to be able to go out for a meal with a Chinese friend, even though they might have been roommates for several months. Months later, when my wife and I were walking through a residential part of Shanghai, we were approached by a young Chinese who clearly wanted to start a conversation with us. But within a minute, he had been arrested by members of the feared Public Security Bureau and led away to who knows what fate.

The Summer Palace was (and still is) a favorite spot for the Chinese themselves. It is hardly surprising this should be so, as the Palace is situated in beautiful grounds. It occupies a couple of square miles, most of which are water. There is a pleasant lake for boating, and islands in the lake to which one can row and take a picnic. In winter, the lake can freeze and people can then go skating. The lake also houses the famous marble boat which the Empress Dowager Tsu His (Cixi) had built out of funds earmarked for the Chinese navy. It is somehow absurd to think that this boat still exists unlike the ships of the British Navy that the Chinese had planned to engage in battle.

The Palace grounds are set among gentle hills. Temples, no

longer functioning as such, are dotted throughout. There is a wonderful long open-sided zig-zagging corridor decorated with scenes from popular Chinese novels of a bygone age. The main hill, Longevity Hill, is only a couple of hundred feet high, on one side of which many of the temples and pagodas are situated. The obverse side of the hill is free of such structures and is a natural and beautiful park. There was also a restaurant whose exorbitant prices made it possible for only the most well-connected cadres to eat there.

Among the crowds who frequented the Palace grounds in the 1970s were some fringe elements. Startled foreigners reported coming across clearly practicing homosexuals, of whom, the official line dictated, there were none in China. In recent years, however, the Chinese have had to admit that homosexuals do exist in China, even (shock, horror) among the Han Chinese themselves. And an interesting change in the meaning of a word has taken place. In the 1970s, it was customary to address people as *tongzhi* (comrade), regardless of their sex, age or status. As China started to open up, however, the meaning of the word *tongzhi* slowly took on a rather different meaning, that of homosexual. This meant the habit of addressing people as *tongzhi* somewhat abated and people started to adopt more traditional forms of address, forms that signaled status and hierarchy. Recently, and perhaps signaling the Party's concern over the development of new hierarchies out of the Party's direct control, the Party has been encouraging people to re-adopt *tongzhi* when referring to or addressing Party officials, despite the secondary meaning of the term.

The fringe elements wandering the grounds of the Summer Palace were not limited to homosexuals. While we were walking through the grounds, my wife suddenly felt her handbag being tugged and her first thought was that someone was trying to steal it. But when she looked down she saw that, in a way, the opposite had occurred, as someone had delivered what looked like a large envelope that was sticking out of a side pocket of her bag. She took the envelope out of her bag and found the Chinese characters for the word *pengyou* (friend) scrawled on it. What to do? We were faced with a dilemma — should we keep the letter or hand it over to Comrade Bi? Was it genuine or was it the work of an agent provocateur testing us? I looked up to find Comrade Bi staring at me through his ridiculous glasses. Had he seen what had happened? I suspected that he had, so I handed over the letter to him. Smile, nervous giggle. And then he rushed off to a colleague and they went off with the letter. Did they find the author of the letter? I don't know. Nothing more was ever said about the incident. Some fifty years on, I still feel a sense of shame at having handed over that letter.

Life at the Institute was not full of adventure and stimulation. As we were all graduates of Chinese, we were marking time at the Institute before it was decided which university we would be sent to. The decision was based on the subject we chose to follow at university, but the kicker was that we did not know which university offered the subject before we decided on it. The choices were history, economics, philosophy and literature. Lyn and I chose literature, which, as I'll relate later, was a lucky choice. While we were waiting to be assigned to our universities, we had to attend language classes. These took place all morning every morning six days a week, and the teacher doled out homework each day. The old, and I had hoped forgotten, feelings I used to have at school when going to class having not done my homework came flooding back.

The classes were terrible. Sentence drills and "repeat after me" formed the basis of most of them. They were, however, better than the Chinese classes a friend and I had taken when visiting

Taiwan a few years earlier during the summer holidays. There the two of us had been seated in a classroom while the teacher – whom we immediately christened 'The Dragon' – ordered us to read some text taken from a Confucian classic. Every time we misread a character – which was not infrequent – the Dragon would bring her wooden ruler down across our knuckles. After two days of this, we upped and left and spent the rest of the holidays truanting around Taiwan.

So, the classes at the Institute were not as bad as that, although the classrooms themselves were not welcoming. Concrete floors, wooden 'school-room' desks, gray walls and a blackboard, pockmarked with cracks. The teachers also adopted curious naming practices. The Chinese names we had been initially assigned were simply transliterations of our full names. As my full name is 'Thomas Andrew Kirkpatrick', this came out as *Tomasi Andelu Kekepatelike*. Fortunately, we were soon able to adopt 'proper' Chinese names. I became *Ke Anzhu*, Being addressed as *Ke Xuesheng* (student *Ke*) was a great deal more comforting than being addressed as *Kekepatelike xuesheng*. *Ke Anzhu* (Peaceful Bamboo *Ke*) remains my Chinese name to this day.

There was also the surprising reincarnation of teacher-student relationships. We had a couple of 'front-row-hands-up' types. The teachers soon decided who were 'good' students and who were 'bad'. The tedium of these classes was one day interrupted by one of our number suddenly emitting a piercing scream. 'I didn't think this class was as bad as that,' I thought to myself. But as the screams continued and heightened in frenzy and volume, it became clear that there was something very seriously wrong. Friends of the distressed girl tried to comfort her and took her out of the classroom. It later transpired that she had been suffering from acute depression for some time, even before she had arrived in China. It had apparently been one of the reasons she had joined us in Beijing rather than meeting us in Hong Kong. The Institute was no place for someone suffering from depression and, mercifully, she was able to fly home.

And then came September 9 and the death of Mao, when all was changed.

6

Four Down Hua to Come

Mao's death not only occasioned grief among the Chinese at the Language Institute. There was also anxiety. And many of the teachers and students had much to be anxious about. The Institute had the reputation, justified, of being a home of the privileged. In China at the time, being privileged, especially as members of the so-called intelligentsia, meant being constantly on guard against a backlash from the left-wing branch of the CCP. While Mao was alive, the Institute was protected by his patronage. Now he was dead, people harbored real fears of an ideological onslaught similar to the one unleashed only a decade or so earlier in the Cultural Revolution. These fears were founded on the belief that many of the leaders, a group comprising Jiang Qing and others, would seize power and reinstitute the reign of terror that characterized the Cultural Revolution. Several of the Institute's lecturers and teachers had suffered during the Cultural Revolution. A university professor with whom I later became great friends told me how he had been stripped, tied to his bed and beaten by his students, while they mocked and criticized him. Many years later, while traveling by train, the Professor slowly realized that the smartly dressed businessman sitting opposite him in the first class railway compartment was one of the students who had stripped and beaten him. He mentioned this to him. The businessman immediately confessed and, incredibly, both apparently then shook hands and agreed to let bygones be bygones.

Many lecturers had also been 'sent down to the countryside' for 're-education through labor' and 'to learn from the peasants'. They did not want to go through such an experience for a second time. This sense of anxiety added to the air of unease and mourning that permeated the campus over the following weeks. Rumors of a vicious power struggle between the leftists and other sections of the CCP were rife, but nothing could be confirmed. Then, a month later, on October 6, we heard on the BBC shortwave news that the infamous Gang of Four, had been arrested. This in itself created a surreal atmosphere. The foreign students had heard that the Gang of Four had been arrested, but no such news had been broadcast by the Chinese media. The Chinese members of the Institute desperately wanted to believe the news but could not, as they had received no confirmation of it from their own official media. Conversations between the foreign students and the Chinese also took on a surreal flavor. On one occasion, just after we had heard the news on the BBC, Wang, a Chinese student of English, wandered unannounced into my room. Wandering unannounced into people's rooms was a habit of Wang's. Far from being a member of the proletariat, Wang was the unreconstructed son of a general and gave himself airs and took great pleasure in ensuring everyone knew he was special. The previous year he had befriended a wealthy student from England who had shown him photos of his country manor house. As I had no photos of country manor houses to show him—a back-to-back terrace in Leeds wasn't quite the same thing—he looked down on me as he would a peasant. He was not blessed with great intelligence and was a poor student of languages. Extraordinarily, however, he had somehow picked up expressions – possibly from the owner of the country manor house – such as 'toodle-pip'. Now, however, he had heard something about the news and was eager to find out more. Discerning this, I teased him.

"So what do you think of the news about Jiang Qing?"

"What news?" he asked, desperately trying to appear disinterested.

"Well, the news about Jiang Qing and the others."

"What news?" he repeated, now displaying a sense of urgency.

"I just wondered whether you had heard anything about their arrests."

This put Comrade Toodle-pip in a tricky position. I had told him news that I knew that he desperately wanted to believe, but could not, unless it was confirmed by official Chinese state media.

"Impossible," he spluttered. "Where did you hear such rubbish?"

"On the BBC."

He now had to continue to pretend not to believe it, as the news had come from a lying mouthpiece of capitalism. He snorted.

"Dog fart! You can't believe such rubbish. When did you hear this bullshit?"

"This morning."

"Dog fart!"

Yet, comrade Toodle-pip found it impossible to maintain an expression of indifference. Despite all the 'dog farts' and the 'bullshit', he actually realized the news might be true. And he was at the forefront when celebrating the downfall of the Gang of Four and ecstatically denouncing them when the Chinese media announced the news a couple of days later.

The official announcement of the arrest of the Gang of Four was greeted with genuine pleasure and relief by most Chinese people. Even the universities of Peking and Tsinghua where Jiang Qing's influence had been high, received the news gladly.

Suddenly, every Chinese you met was keen to tell you how much they had opposed the Gang of Four, and Jiang Qing in particular. This suddenly expressed aversion had its sickening aspect. People like Comrade Toodle-pip who would never have dared — or been so unwise — as to make a public utterance against the leftists now claimed that they had fought against them for years.

"So, if you hated them so much, why didn't you get rid of them earlier?"

Questions such as these were met with expressions of genuine bafflement.

"Because they had power."

Life at the institute picked up after the arrest. The Chinese had been in dire need of something to smile about and now, at last, they had it. Even Comrade Bi started to become talkative and more open. One day he appeared at one of the foreign student's rooms, sat down and led a discussion with us about the Gang of Four. And to be fair to Comrade Bi, although he pointed out that he had known all along what an evil bunch they were, he did not try to suggest, as so many of his compatriots did, that he had been instrumental in their downfall. Rather, he attributed their downfall to incorrectly applying the thoughts of Chairman Mao. This was not an original idea, but Comrade Bi was not one for original ideas. He did concede, however, that, as two of the Gang, Yao Wenyuan and Zhang Chunqiao, had been the Party's ideologues, all the editorials that had been carried in the *People's Daily* and other official newspapers would now have to be re-evaluated. In short, the official line had dissolved. What was confusing now was that, although the current Party line had been abandoned, a new one had not been promulgated. People now did not know quite what to believe or what position to take on any subject. Like the immigrant who arrives in a new country and forgets their first language before learning the new one, the Chinese did not know what to say or how to say it. They stuck to safe ground in denouncing the Gang of Four.

I then asked Comrade Bi a question that reduced him to apoplectic anger. We knew that Taiwan and Tibet—the two Ts— were off limits for rational discussion, but I thought I might ask what I thought to be a fairly straightforward question about Taiwan.

"Do you think there will be a new approach to the Taiwan question?" I asked.

At the mention of the word 'Taiwan'. Comrade Bi's whole demeanor changed. To this point, he had been relatively calm in discussing the fall of the Gang of Four, although somewhat patronizing with his attitude of 'I know you foreigners can't fully understand the situation in China'. But now he suddenly began to shout.

"We must liberate Taiwan!" he cried, his face empurpling with rage.

"Why?"

Comrade Bi was stunned into silence. But not for long.

"You foreigners know nothing of Chinese history!" he raged. "Go and read the history books before you raise this question! Don't insult the Chinese people with your ignorance!"

I felt it would have been churlish to point out that there were no history books that we were actually allowed to consult. He turned to storm out of the room, but not before firing off his parting shot.

"And read the works of Marx, Lenin and Mao!"

With that he slammed the door shut and was gone.

The next interruption to the routine of life came with the news that there was to be a mass rally in Tian An Men square the following Sunday. At the rally, Hua Guofeng, the person credited with arranging the arrest of the Gang of Four, was to be publicly proclaimed the new Chairman of the Communist Party, and therefore the new leader of the People's Republic. The news was greeted with genuine relief and outpourings of real joy. The mass rally was preceded by three days of street parades, three days of gongs, cymbals and drums. Three days of raucous noise as, literally, millions of people paraded through the streets of Beijing. Countless trucks bedecked as floats carried ensembles of exuberant musicians whose primary aim appeared to be to make more noise than anyone else. The cabs of the trucks all carried large portraits of Mao and Hua, with those of Mao far exceeding those of Hua. Behind each lorry came a band of marchers, enveloped in the smoke from the firecrackers that were being constantly let off, adding to the cacophony of sounds. The streets were a mass of red flags being ecstatically waved.

Thursday, the first day of the parades, was the best. The drizzle did nothing to dampen the enthusiasm of the marchers. There was a tangible atmosphere of spontaneous joy, of feelings that had been encaged for so long suddenly breaking free. Bystanders were urged by the marchers to join them. Temporary toilets had been installed by the sides of the streets and suddenly a pack of paraders would dash off to use them and then have to scamper past other groups to rejoin their own.

Groups of children were also part of the parade. While parents were unable themselves to dress colorfully or stylishly, they had splashed out on their children's outfits. Further color was added by the dress of groups of national minorities. Multi-colored skirts and striking headgear.

The spontaneity and exuberance of the Thursday parades gave way on the following two days to much more orderly and restrained battalions of selected marchers representing various work units and institutes. And who was given the honor of leading the Institute's contingent? None other than Comrade Toodle-pip himself.

After three days of parades, it was time for the actual rally itself. Once again, we piled into the fleet of green buses conveying members of the Institute to Tian An Men square—or rather to a point a mile or so from the square from where we had to walk.

The walk from the buses to the square provided an unforgettable experience. Although the rally was not due to start until 3:00 p.m. and it was now only 10:00 a.m., the streets leading to the square were packed with gong-beaters and flag-wavers. The explosive sounds of firecrackers were constant. Our poor teachers had the unenviable task of ensuring that we did not merge with or disappear into some other unit. They operated as primary school teachers overseeing a crocodile of young children. This was an all but impossible task as there were more than one million and a half people heading towards Tian An Men square on that day.

It was therefore an organizational triumph that we arrived in the square as one group and found our way to the area of the square that had been reserved for the Institute. We had been given a prime position as we were in front of the Martyrs' Memorial. This stands in the middle of the square and with it at our backs, we had an uninterrupted view of the Tian An Men 'stage'. Uninterrupted, except for the thousands and thousands of people in front of us.

Then the waiting began. People passed the time by lingering over simple packed lunches, reading, or simply by watching the new arrivals as they poured into the square. Others studied the song sheets we had all been given and attempted to learn the lines. Inevitably, one of the songs was *The East is Red* with its arresting opening lines, "The East is red, the sun is up and China produced a Mao Zedong." Naturally, "The Internationale" was also on the song sheet, but mercifully, this time it would be sung at a more up-tempo pace than it had been during the mourning period.

With several hours of waiting time before the rally would start, there were calls of nature to be made. Providing enough lavatories for the more than a million people who had assembled in the enormous square was clearly a logistical problem of some magnitude. Parts of the square had been set aside to accommodate makeshift loos around which canvas screens had been erected. Visiting the loo was a unique experience. The first task was to find one's way to one of these cordoned-off areas, picking one's way carefully though the mass of bodies and trying to remember the path taken so that one could get back to one's group. On entering, the visitor was met by an extraordinary and never-to-be-forgotten sight. For, although the loos were cordoned off from outside view by the canvas screens, there were no screens of any sort inside. So, after pushing through the canvas flaps of the entrance, one was met by row upon row of naked bottoms, perched, squatting, over long rectangular troughs which were narrow enough so that one could squat over the trough with one foot on either side of it. For those who simply needed a pee – and I am talking about the gents' loos here – one stood on one side of the trough and peed into it. But this proved hard for those of us – myself included – who suffer from what is known as paruresis or shy-bladder syndrome. This can be awkward enough at the best of times, but when one is standing in a long line to pee and facing another long line of pee-ers on the other side of the trough, it becomes something of a challenge. The challenge was heightened immeasurably by the apparent need of the Chinese to inspect the foreigner's equipment, presumably to check if there was anything odd about it. I am still not quite sure how I eventually managed to pee facing a long line of Chinese all of whom seemed to be staring with fascination at a certain part of my anatomy.

If a trip to the loo was a nerve-wracking experience for the males, it was much more so for the females. Reports indicated the females' loos were set up in the same way as the males'. Many westerners are not attuned to or practiced at squatting when going to the loo. Squatting astride a long trench requires balance and dexterity that only years of practice can afford. It is a precarious position to say the least. The result of losing one's balance does not bear thinking about. The girls thus took to going to the loo in pairs, with one holding the hands of the one who was peeing, to ensure there was no overbalancing. The sight of foreigners peeing in pairs in this way naturally occasioned some mirth and ribald comment from the locals.

The rally itself turned out to be something of a damp firecracker. Much of the anticipation of the crowd was generated by the prospect of the new Chairman, Chairman Hua himself, making a speech. Mao had made a speech at a mass rally in Tian An Men in 1949, on the historic occasion of the founding of the People's Republic when he famously announced, "Today, the Chinese people have stood up." Many of those present were confident that Hua would follow suit and say something along the lines of 'Today the Chinese people have stood up once more.' Comrade Bi and colleagues were certain that he would.

As it turned out, not only did Hua not speak, the only person of any consequence who did speak was Wu De, the mayor of Beijing. He was the first to speak, but then, to the increasing annoyance and frustration of the crowd, the next four speeches were made by people who none of the assembled had ever heard of. These speakers were representatives of the various 'classes'. So we were treated to a speech by a worker, a soldier, a member of the Youth League and a woman.

Had we actually been able to hear any of the speeches, I doubt it would have made much difference. But the loudspeaker system, much loved by the authorities as a tool for the broadcasting of propaganda, chose this moment to fail. Sounds were emitted from the loudspeakers, but it was as if someone had attached a scrambling device to the mikes. Cynics felt this was indeed what had happened so that, in later years, the speakers would have the security of there being no record of what they had actually said, just in case the ideological winds shifted and they could be accused of either left- or right-wing deviationism.

After a short while, people stopped trying to decipher what was being said and began instead to talk and grumble among themselves. A million people grumbling is a hell of a grumble. The end of the speeches was greeted with a mass sigh of relief.

The rally was scheduled to conclude with a community singing bash. Holding up our song sheets or straining to see someone else's — some song sheets had been put to use by people visiting the loos — we awaited the opening bars of *The East is Red*. I was looking forward to being part of a choir of a million plus belting out the song. But when the band struck, amazingly, few people sang. There was some half-hearted humming but no full-throated singing. Thus it was for all the three songs on the song sheet.

The singing, or lack of it, was followed by a series of political chants. For these, the chant leader, would scream into the still malfunctioning sound system something along the lines of, 'Long live the great, glorious and correct Communist Party!' or 'Long Live Hua Guofeng!' But even these chants met with little audience response. Most shouted out the 'Long live' part of the chants loudly enough, but whomever or whatever was being wished a long life was mumbled by the masses. In Chinese word order, this comes out as 'mumble mumble mumble, long live'.

The rally had proved an anticlimax for all. But just as we were leaving the square we were provided with some spontaneous entertainment. Some people had formed a small circle and inside the circle were two people, both men, dancing. We watched for a few minutes as the dancers leapt this way and that and, on occasion seemed to start to wrestle to the accompaniment of laughter and shouts of encouragement from the onlookers. Needless to say, we were not to be permitted to watch such spontaneous and unplanned entertainment for long. Our teachers soon put on their primary school hats and suggested, none too subtly, that it was time to leave. We managed to watch for a little longer as the dancers kicked and twisted and bounced in a manner that anticipated break dancing by several years, before succumbing to shepherdly pressure and being herded back to the buses.

On the journey back to the Institute, we held an impromptu post-mortem on the rally. Many of us were surprised that the masses had not joined in any singing and chanting at the end and assumed it was because they were disgruntled that Hua had not spoken. We also felt that Hua had lost an opportunity for gaining a great deal of political capital by not speaking. To have said that the Chinese people had stood up for a second time might have been taking it a bit far, but some exhortatory rhetoric and the promise of better things to come would surely have gone down well. Others felt that it was precisely because Hua might gain huge political capital by speaking that made his colleagues in the leadership ensure he did not speak. But, having since heard Hua speak, it may well have been his embarrassment at his pronunciation of Mandarin that had kept him silent.

7

Urbanities and a Rural Visit

After the rally, life at the Institute reassumed its routine. The classes, although not as deadly as they had been during the period of mourning, never became lively, either. The exception were the General Knowledge classes, which occasionally produced moments of humor, often caused by people struggling with pronunciations across Chinese and English. In one class, the lecturer, in pointing out the "great wisdom" of the Helmsman's (Mao's) thoughts on relating theory to practice, cited the example of Copernicus to give added weight to his argument. He showed how wrong people had been to dismiss Copernicus' theories on the interrelationship between the sun and earth and to assume that Copernicus had a little too much of the former. Misunderstanding arose as the Chinese transliteration of Copernicus comes out as 'Ge Bia Ni Xi' and we were unable to work out who this fellow was. At this moment, the interpreter who attended these classes for just such an eventuality (and to keep tabs on what the lecturer was telling the foreign students) decided she could clear up the confusion. She confidently walked up to the lectern and, rather startlingly, announced in clear tones, "Copper nickers".

A second incident of mispronunciation this time came from

a foreign student mispronouncing Chinese. The class had been asked what elements of Chinese society we would like to see or visit during our stay. This was very much a pro-forma question as we were seldom allowed to see any of the aspects of Chinese society we suggested. On this occasion, one of the students suggested a visit to hear a People's Court in action (this request was, of course, never granted). The Chinese term for People's Court is *renmin fating*. What tickled the audience was that his request came out as, "May we go to hear the people farting?"

Although we never got to see any of the aspects of Chinese society we had requested to see, we did go on some interesting visits. One such was when we toured the underground tunnels that worm for miles under Beijing's streets. They were built to provide shelter, supposedly for the entire population of the city, in the event of an enemy attack, nuclear or otherwise. These tunnels originated in Mao's call to, "Dig tunnels deep, store grain, prepare to defend."

On our visit, the school bus drew up outside what appeared to be a perfectly normal shop in a normal street and in we trooped. The shop assistant, clearly forewarned of our visit, instead of asking something along the lines of 'What can I get you?' or simply grunting, 'Eh?' acted in what must be a relatively unusual manner for a shop assistant. He went behind the counter, momentarily disappeared from view and then his head re-emerged once more and said, "This way, foreign friends," We trooped behind the counter to see that a large wooden trapdoor had been lifted, revealing a yawning blackness beneath.

The tunnels are impressive. They wind for miles underneath the city, and the work that had gone into their construction was staggering. Along the tunnels are side doors that open into rooms, some providing accommodation, some food storage, others electrical generating equipment. They are built for occupants to be self-supporting.

After walking a few hundred yards along a tunnel, we arrived at what looked like the central operations room. We sat at long tables upon which had been placed cups of tea and saucers containing cigarettes. A tunnel spokesman then rose to give us a 'simple introduction' into the workings of the tunnels. A map of the tunnel network was on one of the walls. He pointed at this map with something that looked remarkably like a snooker cue at places on the map as they lit up with little lights. "Now here are the entrances to the tunnels," he said, and a myriad of little lights came on all over the map.

The whole scene recalled one of those British World War II films in which John Mills would invariably play the stoic and brave commanding officer. Our spokesman did not look like John Mills, but he was dressed in uniform and assumed the appropriate manner and tone. These tunnels are real, although one wondered at just how much protection and shelter they would actually provide in the event of an attack. We were assured that the tunnels were all equipped with air purifiers designed to neutralize poison gas if the enemy decided to use it. But it seemed unlikely that this could be so. The tunnels were not very deep either, so we wondered whether they could survive too many direct hits. They were also narrow. It was hard to imagine a scene of anything but chaos if the time came when the population of Beijing had to enter them at the same time.

Although the Chinese organized these occasional outings for foreign students—typically to pay a visit to a factory or to view some film of socialist revolutionary heroism (more on these outings later)—we were also allowed to devise, to a limited extent, our own entertainment. In this respect, Beijing was, at the time, freer than the other major cities. We were, for example, free to leave the city limits and visit the Ming Tombs and the Great

Wall without requiring permission and a permit to do so. It was also possible to cycle out to these places. The journey to the Ming Tombs by bike would take about four hours. One adventurous couple spent the night there. This did occasion severe criticism from the authorities, but apart from criticizing them, no further action — such as repatriation — was taken.

Foreign journalists based in Beijing and members from various embassies would also kindly offer to take foreign students out to these places.

The Ming Tombs are so-called as this is where the tombs or mausoleums of thirteen of the Ming Dynasty (1368-1644) emperors and their wives and concubines are sited. The thirteen tombs are connected by a gun-barrel straight avenue known as the Sacred Way. The Sacred Way is some four miles long and lined with sculptures of guardian animals and officials. Some of the tombs had been restored while others were in varying states of disrepair. They are in a glorious setting at the foot of a mountain range and offer an atmosphere of quiet reflection and a wonderfully welcome escape from the hustle and bustle of Beijing itself. At the time, there were no officials at the tombs and very few visitors, adding to the serenity of setting.

Not all the visitors, however, visited the tombs for a period of quiet reflection and to marvel at the architecture, the Sacred Way with its avenue of animals and the serene setting. One journalist took to driving out there accompanied by several cans of beer and an air rifle. He would first consume the beer and then set up the empty beer cans on stones from a dilapidated tomb and spend a happy hour or two popping away at them with his air rifle.

A trip to the Great Wall was also a favorite outing. On my first visit, I was rather disappointed as only a small section of the wall was open while the rest was in broken disrepair. The part of the wall that was open seemed to be used by the Chinese to gauge the physical fitness of visiting dignitaries, as it is extremely steep in parts. Having had to pause on several occasions in order to regain my breath, I can only admire those elder statesmen who seemed to be able to make it all the way up to the top of the steep incline. It must be an excellent method for investigating the health of visiting heads of state and far less tricky than attempting to sneak off with a urine sample for analysis.

The pleasure of visiting the Great Wall really stemmed from the sense of freedom one could derive from just hopping on a bus and going. We could escape the bureaucratic leash and set out on a journey without having to acquire a travel visa and half a dozen rubber stamps. The feeling of freedom was heightened by the views from the wall on a fine day. You could see for mile upon mile of gently sloping landscape as the hills slowly flattened out to the distant plains. Visiting the Great Wall early in order to be there to greet the dawn, having first procured a bottle of champagne with which to toast the sunrise, was one of life's great pleasures.

Eating out was another source of entertainment and pleasure Beijing afforded the foreigner. This was not because the food was particularly good. At the time, it did not bear comparison with the Chinese food in Hong Kong or even, believe it or not, in Leeds. Those who could afford it — diplomats and the like — could treat themselves to sumptuous banquets. A certain ambassador hosted such a banquet in Shanghai where, rumor had it, each guest ate their way through food that cost the equivalent of the annual salary of the average Chinese. As noted earlier, it is my belief, however, that the more expensive Chinese food is, the less appetizing it is. This may be because of the long-standing Chinese tradition that the best things in life must be the rarest or most difficult to procure. When it comes to food, it is the bear's paw that is the delicacy. Chinese diners are ecstatic at the prospect of eating sturgeon's bowel. An herb that can be found only in impossibly inaccessible parts of darkest Tibet must therefore be *the* herb to enhance the flavor of food.

But there were many restaurants that were worth visiting, some in splendid surroundings, from cheap dumpling places in parks to a Muslim restaurant overlooking a lake. Perhaps the most luxurious was the restaurant housed in what used to be the home of Yuan Shikai, the warlord who assumed the presidency of China from 1912 to 1915. This apparently became the favorite restaurant of Deng Xiaoping. And then there was the restaurant by the zoo that we referred to as the 'Moscow' as it had been the Soviet Exhibition Hall until the Soviets left after their alliance with Mao and the CCP foundered in the early 1960s. Luckily, they left their vodka behind them and this was still served at the 'Moscow' restaurant. We had been able to enjoy the vodka on our visits to the Moscow during our time at the Institute, but when we returned to Beijing in 1977, we were dismayed to discover that it had run out. But it was not just the vodka that attracted foreigners to The Moscow. It was set up as a western restaurant. There were linen table cloths and silver cutlery. It had high-domed ceilings, candelabras and ornate furnishings. It also served ice cream in silver ice cream cups.

And then there were the restaurants that catered for the 'people' or the 'masses'. These were cheap, solid good home cooking — where the 'home' could be one of a provincial cuisine such as Sichuan or Hunan — and were invariably incredibly crowded. They were, naturally enough, very popular with the foreign students, not least because they provided a rare opportunity, if not exactly to mingle with the masses, but at least to eat alongside them in the same restaurant. They were, in the main, shunned by members of the diplomatic corps, but foreign journalists liked to frequent them in the hope they might overhear titbits of conversations criticizing the regime.

Because these restaurants were cheap and lively, they provided the foreign students with a most welcome means of escaping the regimented existence of the Language Institute. After a day trying to repress the desire to thump Comrade Bi, a trip to a masses restaurant helped preserve sanity and re-calibrate perspective. As the mind relaxed with the first soothing drafts of beer, it became possible to remember that the great majority of Chinese were not CCP cadres but simple good-hearted people who enjoyed good food and a few beers.

A further reason for seeking solace and eating out in local restaurants was the alternative: eating in. The institute boasted three canteens, namely 'Chinese', 'Western' and 'Muslim'. In fact, the food in the Western canteen was pretty good, if monotonous. But being a canteen it had all the disadvantages of canteens, the most glaring one being the need to queue. Queues are tedious at the best of times, even when orderly and people understand the concept of sequence – which entails the understanding that the person in front of you will get served before you do. This concept is drilled into the British virtually from birth. People stand in line and wait their turn. You join a queue by going to the back of it. But this concept is not a cultural universal. To many, a queue is something to get to the front of as quickly as possible. As the foreign student body was made up of people from many different cultures, many with different attitudes to the concept of the queue, queueing became an exercise in defending one's place in it from people who would simply attempt to insert themselves towards the front of the queue. Outraged shouts of "You must line up!" provided a common soundtrack to the frequent scuffles that broke out in these 'queues'. One foreign student took to arriving at the queue holding a microphone and recorder and recording the events that were unfolding before him.

"I am now standing in the queue in the Western dining hall of the Beijing Language Institute," he would portentously intone.

"The queue is made up of some twenty foreigners, and seems to be moving in an orderly manner. Certainly, as yet there has been no attempt to gate-crash the queue by members of those nationalities who appear to need to eat before others."

To my continued amazement, no one ever tried to snatch the microphone out of his hand and tell him in no uncertain terms to bugger off.

On occasion, one was rewarded for eating in the Institute canteens by the unlikely sight of Comrade Bi serving. Members of the cadre class were required to undertake bouts of what was called 'Open Door Schooling'. This required them to do some manual labor so that they might be able to re-identify with the masses, which is to say the peasants, workers and soldiers. Open Door Schooling was also required of the foreign students and I relate my experiences of it later. I must say, I found it something of an uplifting to experience to be faced with a smiling Comrade Bi and his teeth as I went to a serving hatch to collect my meal. Perhaps they should introduce some form of Open Door Schooling to the British House of Commons.

An alternative to eating in the Western canteen was to try the Chinese one. There, the word queue took on a different meaning for all. In the Chinese dining hall, the diner did not so much join the queue so much as the queue joined the diner. The prospective diner would get jostled forward in a scrum of arms and elbows amid an incessant din of people shouting to one another across the hall, and of hundreds of spoons clanging against chipped enamel bowls.

Eventually, the diner would find himself at a serving window and it was here that the problems really began. He first had to order the amount of rice he wanted—rice was dispensed in units known as '*liang*' with one *liang* being equivalent to fifty grams. He then, in a raised voice to make himself heard against the cacophony of clanging spoons and shouts, told the harassed servers what he wanted, whether this was bean curd soup, pork and black beans or whatever. This was no easy matter as the specialist argot of the dining hall was unfamiliar. Then came the real test, the test that sorted out the experienced Chinese dining hall person from the mere visitor: paying for the meal. For this purpose, meal tickets were issued. Meal tickets were also used for paying for meals in the Western canteen. But to add a little trepidation and insecurity to the diner, each canteen required different tickets. In the Chinese canteen, there were tickets for grain—rice, noodles and bread products such as steamed buns—and tickets for the different types of main dishes. Following the law concerning tickets of this nature, it was almost always impossible to select a hand of tickets that added up exactly to the amount of the dishes bought. This was tricky when our diner noticed in dismay that, while having ordered pork and black beans, a bowl of bean curd soup had been brought to the serving hatch in its stead. Having prepared to pay for the pork and beans, our diner now had to feverishly flick through the book of tickets (which were about the size of a match box) to try and tear off tickets amounting to the required sum for bean curd soup rather than pork and beans (for which he had been congratulating himself for having torn off the right number of tickets). It took exceptional *sang froid* not to become discombobulated on these occasions. Even if one had been in the calm precincts of a library where one could concentrate fully on working out the number of tickets and of which sort were required, it would present a formidable task. When being jostled relentlessly by fellow diners and amid the cacophony and the hubbub of clanging spoons, screeching chairs, raised voices and the server calling impatiently the equivalent of 'Four *liang* of rice and bean curd soup', it became next to impossible.

So, procuring food in the Chinese canteen was an unnerving experience. Often the shy and sensitive simply gave up and decided, with heads bowed, to make for the Western canteen with the inner conviction they had failed in some way. Those who managed to work the system and procure food were now faced with their next challenge: finding somewhere to sit. Needless to say, this was not easy. There are many expressions available for describing the Chinese dining hall but not many are as apt 'a trifle overcrowded'.

Our diner, having miraculously managed to collect his four *liang* of rice and bean curd soup supper, would with an enamel bowl of rice in one hand and an enamel bowl of bean curd soup in the other, and with spoon clenched between his teeth, anxiously survey the dining hall looking for somewhere to sit. His anxiety was not simply caused by the fear of not finding a place but also by the fact that the enamel bowls proved to be admirable conductors of heat. Whatever faults it may have had as a soup per se, the bean curd soup was served scaldingly hot. As a consequence, our diner, having cast urgent glances around the room trying to gauge who among the multitude of diners was likely to finish soon and free up a seat, suddenly lurched towards the nearest table and crashed his bowl of soup down upon it, thereby splashing a quantity of it onto his fingers. The splash was followed by an oath, cut off in its prime by the plunging of his scalded fingers into his mouth.

Eventually, he succeeded in finding a spot and sat down to eat his lunch. On taking the first spoonful of what remained of his bean curd soup, he slowly became aware of a voice nearby that was not speaking Chinese. With a sinking heart and knowing what this might forebode, he would look up to see a face grinning inanely at him. 'You speak English?' the grinner asked.

This proved the final straw. Feeling guilty for not encouraging an impromptu English lesson, our diner muttered a brief apology and scurried out of the dining hall, leaving his rice and soup virtually untouched.

This may seem to have been unconscionably rude, but we were driven to it by the incessant desire of the Chinese students of English to engage us in conversation at every opportunity. It didn't help when these interactions often started with the Chinese student announcing proudly, "Thanks to our great and glorious leader and the Party, I am studying English."

I'm afraid to say I later learned to deflect these requests for impromptu English lessons by saying, "I am so sorry but I come from Iceland and cannot speak English." This was a successful strategy as the Chinese had no idea where Iceland was and accepted what I was saying at face value. (And this comes with an apology to the Icelandic students at the Institute, both of whom spoke flawless English).

The ambition of most foreign students at the Language Institute was to get out of it. Those of us who had arrived in Beijing with a degree in Chinese from their home countries stood a good chance of escaping and moving to a university within two or three months of arrival. When you got sent to a university depended upon the subject you had elected to study and, as I noted earlier, you had to select the course of study before knowing which university would be offering it. For second world students, there was not a wide choice of subjects available. In 1976, these were limited to Economics, History, Language, Literature and Philosophy. There were also exceptional cases of students from the second world studying Traditional Chinese Medicine. Generally speaking, however, medicine and science subjects were the preserve of the third world students, with medicine, engineering and textiles being the three most popular subjects. As the third word students had arrived in China with no knowledge of Chinese, they had to spend at least one year at the Institute. As recorded above, the poor man who had been volunteered by his father, the Ambassador, took three years before he was allowed to proceed to the university.

Lyn and I, along with two other English students, had elected to study literature. We then had to wait patiently until we got to hear where and when we would be going.

Towards the end of October, I was summoned by Comrade Bi to take a phone call from our man at the British Embassy. He had just received a letter from the Ministry of Education concerning the first placement of British students.

"Well?" I asked, conscious of a slight tightening of the stomach and clenching of the bowel. After all, this could be portentous news affecting the rest of our time in China.

"Mixed news," he announced. 'Five of you are going to Shenyang but you are not one of them."

Actually, as far as I was concerned, this was good news all round. The five who had chosen language as their course of study were the ones going to Shenyang. That meant those of us who had chosen to study literature would not be going there. Shenyang is an important industrial town and the capital of Liaoning Province in northeast China. I have never been to Shenyang, but have visited the northeastern cities of Harbin and Changchun in winter when the temperatures hovered around a refreshing minus thirty degrees. I was bearded at the time and after only ten minutes outside, I could snap off bits of frozen beard. Pinching one's nostrils caused eye-watering pain as the frozen nostril hairs pierced the nasal tissue. And that was when there was good heating and the cities were prosperous and food plentiful. But when it was thirty degrees below in 1970s Shenyang, which it was for most of the winter months, the students were barricaded in the same building where they slept, ate and studied. Reports from the students who were allocated to Shenyang also complained about the food, or lack of it. Shenyang has never been a center of Chinese cuisine, far from it. Tired and withered cabbage leaves formed the staple. And, while there were restaurants in town, the sight of 'big-nosed' 'foreign friends' was so rare that the students attracted a crowd of spectators wherever they went, including restaurants. Eating out, therefore, was a very tiresome exercise. They say Shenyang gets better in the summer: it would have to.

In total, fifteen students had been selected to go to Shenyang and they were told they would be leaving the following week. The news was not received rapturously. Indeed, several students snorted their refusal to go. (In a previous year, one British student had barricaded himself into his room at the Institute on learning that he was to be sent to Shenyang.) However, when the day of departure arrived, all fifteen presented themselves packed and ready to go.

Packing was an art in itself. On arrival in China, each foreign student was presented with:

wash basin, enamel, 1

flask, thermos, 1

mattress, under, 1

quilt, 1

blanket, 1

These items stayed with the students wherever they might be sent and were to be returned to the authorities on their departure from China.

While it might appear there must be many ways of packing a quilt, under mattress and blanket, in China there is only one correct way of performing this task. Sadly, throughout my stay in China I never managed to unravel its mysteries (I still struggle when trying to put on a fresh duvet cover and somehow often find myself flailing around helplessly, somehow having managed to make my way inside the cover.) It was fascinating to watch the Chinese, steeped in the art, as they packed their quilts, mattresses and blankets in under ten minutes and produced a bundle that not only looked neat but was easy to carry. It was somewhat embarrassing, on the other hand, to struggle in vain to produce something similar under the disdainful eye of the experts. My completed bundle always looked as though it was something that needed packing rather than something that had just been packed. Happily, other foreign students clearly had the same problem with their bundles. The sadness of saying farewell to the group, which had become known as the 'Shenyang Fifteen,' was somewhat tempered by the sight of fifteen bundles packed by people, all of whom seemed to have graduated from a school that encouraged expression through the use of free forms.

As we waited in the pleasant October evening for the bus that was to deliver the Shenyang fifteen to the railway station, we tried to strike a carefree tone and made inane remarks along the lines of, 'I'm sure it can't be as bad as they say,' all said with complete lack of conviction. At this moment, an extremely flustered-looking Comrade Bi appeared. He glanced at apparent disbelief at the bundle collection. He was clearly hot and bothered and was in something approaching a panic as he urged the students to board their bus. Poor Comrade Bi may well have had an inkling that allowing only thirty minutes to get to the station and catch the train was cutting things a little fine.

Several hours later, the bus returned to the Institute with all passengers still on board. Much to Comrade Bi's chagrin, they had missed the train. Chagrin had soon given way to humiliation.

On realizing that they had missed the train, Comrade Bi began to behave like someone from an old silent movie, walking around and gesticulating at several frames a second. In his panic he even suggested the group dash through the night in a bus after the train in an attempt to catch up with it. To the grave disappointment of the Shenyang Fifteen, who rather fancied the excitement of a night time dash, this plan was immediately vetoed by someone with more sense and authority.

Comrade Bi's humiliation was not eased by the knowledge that he had blotted his copybook and would have to face the unpleasant consequences of so doing. More time at the canteen's serving hatch, for example. And then he also had to face the not insignificant problems of rebooking tickets to Shenyang for fifteen foreign students. In those days, one simply did not breeze up to the station ticket office and say "15 singles to Shenyang, please." There were obstacles to be overcome, hurdles to be cleared, before one arrived at the ticket buying stage. First, a travel permit was needed. Travel permits were issued by the China Travel Service. The China Travel Service issued permits about as readily as a bank manager issuing overdrafts to someone using a 'cert' in the 3:30 p.m. at Doncaster as collateral. And, in the case of foreign students, the China Travel Service needed permission from the Ministry of Education before it would issue permits or tickets. A further complication resided in the nature of the travel permits themselves. These not only specified the exact date upon which the person could travel, but also specified which train was to be taken. A travel permit, then, only allowed the holder to buy a particular ticket for a particular train leaving a particular station at a particular time. And that was not all. It specified the particular time and place of destination. In short there were a hell of a lot of particulars involved in getting permission for fifteen foreign students to travel by train. So, missing the train presented a number of problems.

On his return to the Institute, Comrade Bi went into full overdrive. And, to his credit, he somehow managed to get the tickets for the fifteen poor souls who were due to travel to Shenyang the following day re-allocated to the Shenyang Fifteen. They were therefore able to leave only twenty-four hours behind schedule.

Comrade Bi spent the next ten days down on a commune. This spell in the country, however, had not been meted out as punishment for his Shenyang blunder, but was all part of the CCP's general scheme of things. The time had come for us all to be given our first taste of what was known as 'Open Door Schooling'.

8

'OPEN DOOR SCHOOLING' AND EVERGREEN COMMUNE

'Open Door Schooling' was the nationwide system under which students and those souls classified as 'intellectuals' spent a period of time studying from soldiers in the army, from workers in a factory and from peasants on a people's commune. A people's commune was an amalgamation of collective farms which, in addition to agricultural pursuits, also administered the villages. These communes were first set up in the late 1950s. The idea behind the 'Open Door Schooling' scheme was to give pampered university students and intellectuals -- a much distrusted and despised class in China at the time -- a taste of what life was really like for workers, peasants and soldiers. The idea was an excellent one, but like so many such ideas in China, the gulf between the idea and its implementation, between theory and practice, was enormous.

The first problem was that there was simply too much of it. In 1976, for example, some students spent as much as three months of the academic year in open door schooling. As a consequence, their academic work suffered.

The second problem was that many of the students being required to learn from the soldiers, workers and peasants were actually soldiers, workers or peasants themselves. As intellectuals were not trusted, the CCP had opened university study to people from those members of the proletariat who could be trusted, namely soldiers, workers and peasants. Comrade 'Toodle-pip' was not a typical Institute student, most of whom came from the 'preferred' classes. But it was clearly absurd to send someone who had grown up on a people's commune back to one to learn from the peasants. What such a person really needed was time to focus on university study.

The third problem was that, although the students were supposed to participate in the work where they had been sent, when they got to the commune or factory, in many instances, they did not work at all. For example, in 1977, when the Chinese students from the Chinese Department of prestigious Fudan University in Shanghai spent a month's 'Open Door Schooling' on a commune, they actually worked on only seven of those thirty days. The other twenty-three days were spent indulging in a favourite CCP pastime: holding meetings. Needless to say, the sight of a bunch of students who had arrived at the commune supposedly to help out in the fields sitting around in what looked like idle chatter did not go down well with the peasants. Rather than serving to forge a link between the intellectual and the peasant, Open Door Schooling served to widen the gap between them.

Whatever purpose 'Open Door Schooling' served for the Chinese students, foreign students would look forward to it. It provided a most welcome break from the tedium of life at the Institute and learning how a commune operated and working alongside peasants sounded as though it would be an interesting and rewarding experience. So, we were all looking forward to our ten-day stay at Evergreen Commune.

Evergreen Commune

Perhaps I should have expected it, having lived in China for a couple of months by this stage, but I had not envisaged life on the commune to start each day with 'morning discussions'. Doing a bit of digging, planting a seed or two perhaps, but not a morning discussion. These morning discussions should more accurately be called 'monologues', as they were characterized by speeches delivered by various commune spokesmen — and they were always men. After the speeches a few questions would be allowed but seldom answered. None of the commune spokesmen could ever be mistaken for gifted orators. Each speech followed the same pattern — a pattern which was to be repeated in speeches wherever we were visiting, be it commune or factory. They were also given in rooms of tired similarity with faded brown being the predominant color of the overall decor. Often we would be seated at a long table with the spokesman at the head. Along the length of the table would be arranged saucers or rectangular bowls filled with an expensive brand of local filter-tipped cigarettes, of which we were incessantly encouraged to partake. In front of each place there would be a large ceramic cup, covered with a lid, and filled with Chinese tea. The cups would be constantly topped up by drably uniformed women, often no more than girls, hovering behind the seats, and carrying large kettles of boiling water. On occasions when we visited somewhat grander places, such as a government institution, we would be given large ornate armchairs in which to sit. These invariably had wooden arms the width of a book and headrests draped with large white antimacassars. Once cigarettes were lit and the first sips of tea taken, the spokesman announced he was about to begin by a loud clearing of his throat accompanied by alarming hacking sounds emanating from his chest and then turning to spit, with happy accuracy, an amalgam of gob and spittle, which made a satisfyingly resounding smack as it splattered against the inner rim of nearby spittoon.

All the spokesman had been taught the same framework for the speech, which went something like this:

"Welcome to our humble commune, international students. Today I would like to give you a simple introduction to our commune. Before the liberation, the standard of living of our Chinese peasants was very low. But after liberation, the standard of living of our Chinese peasants increased. Before the Great Leap Forward movement of the 1950s, the standard of living of our peasants remained relatively low. But after the Great Leap Forward movement, the standard of living of our Chinese peasants improved a little. (Here he might pause and turn, noisily bring up another globule of phlegm and spit it smack bang into the middle of the spittoon and then resume.) Before the Great Proletarian Cultural Revolution, the standard of living of our Chinese peasants remained relatively low. But after the Great Proletarian Cultural Revolution, the standard of living of our Chinese peasants increased once more. Before the Criticize Confucius and Criticize Lin Biao campaign, the standard of living of our Chinese peasants was still relatively low. But after the Criticize Confucius and Criticize Lin Biao campaigns, the standard of living of our Chinese peasants increased a little. And now, thanks to the thought of Mao Zedong, the standard of living of our peasants has increased exponentially. Agricultural production increased by more than 50 percent between 1968 and 1973. The 1976 harvest showed an increase of 14.3 percent over the 1975 harvest. If anyone has any questions, please raise them." Another resounding smack as more phlegm hit the spittoon.

We soon learned that asking questions was a frustrating exercise, as concrete answers were impossible to obtain. The spokesmen talked entirely in terms of percentages, never in real figures, so one had no idea what the percentages being given really meant. And any question or comment that was considered contrary to the spirit of the occasion such as, "We had heard that, rather than improving the life of the peasants, the Great Leap Forward had actually led to the starvation of millions" would be met with the same rehearsed answer. The spokesman would sigh and respond in the most patronizing of tones, "Ah, you foreign international students probably do not fully understand the situation in our country."

The only time the spokesman got really riled by an impertinent question was when one of the Swiss students asked, "How does this thing you call Mao Zedong Thought increase the peasants' standard of living?"

This not only raised the ire of the spokesman, as to question the all-round beneficial effects of Mao Zedong Thought was tantamount to blasphemy, but to call Mao Zedong thought 'a thing' was the gravest insult imaginable. The response that we "probably didn't fully understand the situation in our country" was uttered with some venom, whereupon the spokesman closed the meeting.

These speeches had two major effects upon those unfortunate enough to have to sit through them. The initial irritation at being unable to cut through the rehearsed waffle and unearth any concrete information was followed by apathy coated with a heavy cloak of ennui.

That the speeches soon became boring goes without saying. Not only did each spokesman say more or less the same thing, they said it in the same way and using the same language. Every noun or name had an adjective that had to be used with it. In 1976, Mao was always 'great', Hua Guofeng 'wise' and the CCP 'great, glorious and correct'. Harvests were always 'abundant'. These descriptives can only be changed by official diktat, at the command of the Central Committee. So a drought-ridden harvest is abundant until otherwise directed from above. For example, harvests that had been described as 'abundant' in 1976, were to be called 'sabotaged' in 1977 on orders of the CCP. In early 1976, Deng Xiaoping had to be referred to as a 'counter revolutionary element'. By the end of the year he had miraculously become 'a good comrade'. Thus, does universal truth occasionally allow some slippage.

The morning discussions over, it was time for lunch. Not, however, a lunch made from fresh produce grown on the commune to which we had all been fervently looking forward after two months of Institute canteen food. Our disappointment was tangible—and somewhat forcefully expressed by some— when we discovered that lunch had been transported from the Institute canteen. Not only did this mean we could not eat the local food, but also we could not mingle with the locals, as the lunch was a meal ticket affair and only for the foreign students. The lunches provided for us while we were at the commune could not be called appetizing. It was as if the van bringing the lunch had had to break suddenly and then accelerate, causing the food it was transporting to become merged as one—indecipherable bits of meat in a slushy sauce.

Lunch over, it was time for a nap or, as the Chinese say, it was 'xiuxi' time. The Chinese are true gold medallists when it comes to napping. Most seem able to nap anywhere at any time. On one memorable night I was playing billiards in very dimly lit billiard hall in a less than salubrious district of Beijing and felt the need to pee. As was almost always the case, the WC was outside—a concrete rectangle with no roof or doors; just an entry way leading to a trough for peeing in and a series of four or five holes with footrests on either side of them for more serious activity. Gentlemen were squatting over three of the holes. As it was pitch dark, all they could tell was that someone had come in; they could not see that it was a foreigner. While I was occupied, I could hear them chatting when, one of them suddenly burst into laughter on realizing that the reason that there had been no contribution to the repartee from one of his colleagues was because he had fallen asleep on the squat.

"Old Li's dropped off!" he guffawed, loudly enough to wake Old Li from his reverie.

As I said, the Chinese could nap pretty well anywhere and at any time. But there was also a rigorously observed nap time or siesta period taken after lunch. Lunch was eaten early in China, typically before noon, and lunch was always followed by a *xiuxi*. This could last for as long as two hours and there was absolutely no point in trying to get anything done or to see anyone on official business during this time. A few years later, I was on an official visit to a tertiary institution in the northeast of China. I arrived just after lunch. I was somewhat taken aback to be promptly escorted across the campus by an extremely attractive teacher to one of the halls of accommodation, showed into a single room which was equipped with a comfortable bed and told to "*xiuxi* for two hours."

After a morning trying not to nap through speeches, picking at an uninspiring lunch and having a nap, it was time to actually do some manual work. But to say we worked hard during our time at Evergreen Commune would be to stretch the truth. Our time was divided between some desultory digging, removing ears of corn from their husks and eating the excellent apples that were the pride of the Commune's produce. This was also a time when we had the opportunity to chat to the locals. Sadly, however, attempts at conversation were hampered by the locals' inability to understand the way we foreigners spoke Chinese and our inability to decipher the Mandarin being spoken by the peasants, as it came heavily accented and with a good dose of the local dialect. In 1976, very few Chinese had had the opportunity to hear foreigners speak Mandarin. The idea that foreigners might actually be able to speak their language was also incredible to most. So our attempts to converse were often met with looks of stunned incredulity. I was reminded of a story recounted to me by a Japanese-speaking colleague who, on chatting happily with some Japanese farmers in a rural part of Japan was startled to hear one of them say (in Japanese),

"You know. It's very strange. English must be very similar to Japanese. We can understand almost everything you say!"

There was also a certain amount of shyness on both sides. That the locals were shy was only to be expected. Every afternoon at 2:00 p.m., a group of foreign students would descend on them to 'help' them in the fields and promptly at 5:00 p.m., be whisked off again, not to be seen again until the following afternoon. It is safe to say that our first attempt at 'Open Door Schooling' was not a resounding success. This was a shame for, as we learned when we went to live on a commune for a couple of weeks the following summer, working and living on a commune was an extremely rewarding experience, as will be related later.

9

RIDING AN AMBASSADOR

After five days of to-ing and fro-ing between the Institute and
Commune Evergreen, the four British students who had elected
to study literature were told we would be going to Fudan
University in Shanghai. We breathed a huge sigh of relief, as
Fudan and Shanghai had the reputation of being by far the best
of the available billets. It was also touching to see how pleased
our Chinese teachers were for us, when they found out that
Lyn and I had been posted to the same university. It was also
a reminder that couples in China are routinely separated by
the State according to the perceived needs of the State. Many
Chinese couples only got to see each other once a year over the
annual Spring Festival marking the Chinese New Year.

We spent the remainder of our time in Beijing making
preparations for the move to Shanghai and going out on farewell
binges with friends we had made in Beijing. Lyn and I were
both happy to be leaving Beijing in general and the Language
Institute in particular. Happy to be leaving the Institute to escape
its claustrophobic tedium and happy to be leaving Beijing as it
was an easy place to slip into a social scene with other foreigners,
students, diplomats and journalists. This was becoming
expensive — among other things I was running up a formidable

tab at the British Embassy pub, The Bell. Each Friday evening, an embassy van would collect the British students from the Institute and take us to the Bell where, for a couple of hours — sometimes longer — we could imagine we were back in a pub in England as we played darts and downed pints. This was a very thoughtful gesture on the part of the Embassy, as it gave all of us a chance to vent our frustrations and feel were not as isolated as we often felt while at the Institute.

The British Embassy had also laid on a welcome party for us soon after our arrival, hosted by the Ambassador himself, Edward Youde. He seemed typically straight-laced and stiff-upper lipped, but was a brilliant sinologist and a highly effective diplomat who went on to become governor of Hong Kong. Had I been considering a career pathway in the British Foreign Office, it might have met with a bump when the Ambassador discovered me in the Embassy kitchens rooting around a large fridge in a vain search for beer. I had been driven to this action as the welcoming party had only run to a single glass of the stuff for each guest. The contrast between the British and Australian ambassadors at the time could hardly have been starker. I had become friendly with an Australian diplomat, and Lyn and I were invited to attend Melbourne Cup day at the Australian Embassy. In Australia, the Melbourne Cup is a horse race run on the first Tuesday in November and is always referred to as 'the cup that stops a nation'. It certainly stopped work at the Australian Embassy that evening. The Australian Ambassador, Stephen Fitzgerald, was, like his British counterpart, a brilliant sinologist, but unlike his British counterpart, straight laced he was not; and, in Australian parlance, he enjoyed his grog. There was no shortage of beer on offer. For the Melbourne cup the Australians had devised a game. A number of lanes had been marked off on the floor of a large hall, with each lane comprising a number of squares, also marked. These lanes represented the race track. Now, horses, trainers and riders were needed. There were determined by each person present drawing a ticket out of a hat. The ticket informed the person who had drawn it whether they were a horse, a trainer or a rider. The trainer and rider tickets also carried the name of the relevant horse. I drew a jockey's ticket, Lyn a trainer's. Then the fun begun. The 'horses' knelt on all fours at the start of their respective lane, with the 'jockey' sitting astride their back. The trainer would roll a die to determine how many squares the horse could advance. This was done horse by horse so that the trainers took it in turns to roll the dice. The winner was, of course, the horse and rider that made it to the finishing line first. The race was accompanied by shouts of laughter, people urging horses to put on some pace and an extraordinary sense of gaiety. I don't think there can be many people who can claim to have ridden an Australian Ambassador, but I was drawn as the Ambassador's jockey. As far as I can remember, we finished a creditable fourth, just out of the places. I still chuckle when I recall that evening, especially when I consider the likelihood of Sir Edward Youde (he was knighted in 1977) being happy to kneel on all fours and be ridden by a foreign student of a jockey.

That is not to say that the British Embassy was completely devoid of a sense of humor. When it was discovered that I had been in Taiwan the previous year when the President of the so-called Republic of China, Chiang Kai-shek, had died, and it was realized that Chairman Mao had encountered the same fate not long after I had arrived in Beijing, one member of the diplomatic corps remarked,

"You wouldn't fancy hopping down to Singapore for us would you? We're having a bit of trouble with the chap in charge down there."

10

To Shanghai and Fudan University

Fudan University had sent two lecturers to chaperone us on our journey south. They could hardly have been more different. One was a petite thin female of an indeterminate age, but on the far side of forty. She exuded an air of stuffy self-satisfaction, not entirely deserved. She proved adept at answering questions without providing information of any value. She was the sort of person, on being asked where Shanghai was, would reply, 'China'. Her companion chaperone was a different proposition entirely. He was a comfortably plump, but tall male, with an open and affable face. The sort of person who would be among the first asked to play Father Christmas. Perhaps the rather alarming noises that suggested a hard line struggle was taking place in the vicinity of his navel might have disqualified him. He introduced himself as the person in charge of the classical literature course and was the first academic I had met in China who openly displayed enthusiasm for his subject. He informed us, in between scarcely disguised belches and burps, that there were two Chinese literature courses open to foreign students at Fudan, namely Modern Chinese Literature and Classical Chinese Literature. He did not seem the slightest bit put out when only one of us indicated that he would opt for the classical course.

Had we known what was coming in the Modern Literature Course, most of us would have opted for the classical course, too.

Painfully aware that my bundle of bedclothes looked as though burglars had tried to unravel it, we boarded the bus to take us to the station. Comrade Bi had learned his lesson and we arrived in plenty of time. While on the bus, I surveyed my fellow students. We were very much a job lot made up of four English, a few French, a Belgian, a Swede, a Norwegian, an Australian and a German. It was the German that captured my attention, as I could not recall ever having seen him before. He would have been difficult to overlook. He was tall, had a full beard and might have been good-looking had his face been more carefully assembled. On his head sat a fur hat. His bundle was immaculate. His luggage also boasted a snazzy aluminium trunk. He gave off a slightly sinister, knowing air.

I spent the rest of the bus journey reflecting on what we had witnessed and experienced since our arrival in Beijing a little more than two months earlier. Chairman Mao had died and we had attended the Lying in State. The Gang of Four had been 'smashed' and Hua Guofeng installed as the new Chairman. We had attended the mass rally of more than a million in Tian An Men Square celebrating this fact. We had not been sent to Shenyang, but instead to Shanghai. We were escaping the sterility of the Language Institute to attend one of the most prestigious universities in China. I had acted as jockey to the Australian Ambassador's horse. It had been quite a couple of months with the account, I felt, happily in the black.

We traveled by second-class sleeper on the train to Shanghai. These second-class sleeper carriages comprised sixty bunks arranged in ten sets of six in what might be considered open plan, as there were no doors. Each carriage also had a couple of wash basins, a hot water urn and a squat lavatory, which did have a door.

Being classified as 'honored foreign friends', we were allowed to take our meals in the first-class dining room. This was an extraordinary privilege, as the food was excellent and cold beer available and a significant mark up from the second-class provisions. The locals, being in second class, received an aluminium tin full of rice with meat and vegetable trimmings. These tins were delivered by a chap pushing and rattling a rickety old and wobbly trolley up and down the corridor (the space between the serried rows of bunks and the side of the carriage). He would periodically croak, "Food, food," A few minutes later, he would come rattling back to collect the empty tins.

My main memory of the trip is of noise. In addition to the incessant din that sixty travelers make in a door-less carriage and the noise of the train itself, there was one source of noise that outdid all the others and this was the noise emanating from the loudspeakers. Ranks of loudspeakers lived along the ceiling of each carriage and at each end of them. Seasoned travelers avoided the top bunks from which the ceiling loudspeakers were a mere foot or so away. To be awakened at six in the morning by martial music followed by a Chinese female screeching at maximum volume was not only unnerving but annoying in the extreme. It was not as if the loudspeaker was transmitting news of any interest. The traveler would be informed of the apparently vital news that Comrade X from carriage Y was this week's master carriage cleaner. Then there would be a quote or several from the works of Chairman Mao. Then general advice along the lines that it would be wise to take the precaution of boarding a train before it was due to leave the station. Constant martial music, quotes, anodyne news and advice. All from six in the morning until 10:00 p.m. at night. And there was no way of turning the bloody thing off.

The journey itself was relatively uneventful. One of our number, something of a master at Chinese chess, spent much of the journey playing against fellow travelers. Chinese chess, indeed chess in China, was played according to a very different set of rules of etiquette than those observed in the West. For example, an observer offering frequent and urgent advice for a player's next move while leaning over the player's shoulders would be severely frowned upon at home. In China this was normal and bystanders would offer a continuous stream of suggestions about which piece to move and where. Enthusiastic bystanders could not only proffer advice but could actually personally move the particular piece to where they felt it should go. Players who ignored crowd advice and elected to move their pieces according to their own designs would be greeted with collective snorts of derision and mock despair after each move. Chess in China was therefore more of a team sport, a team that any interested passer-by could join.

When we arrived in Shanghai, the German, whom I shall call K, did his reputation no harm at all by being met by an attractive European female who seemed deliriously happy to see him. She was clearly from a culture that encouraged self-expression as she expressed her feelings by throwing her arms around him and showering him with kisses in a show of abandonment that had the Chinese averting their gaze with embarrassment and us gawping with astonishment. K accepted this welcome as though it was his right and only to be expected. I was a little relieved to discover later that they had met in China the previous year and that it was not a case of lust or love at first sight.

11

'STUDENTS IN CHINA CANNOT BE MARRIED!'

Before we had left Beijing, Lyn and I had been warned we would not be permitted to live together. But we had also been told that we would be sharing rooms with Chinese students from the Chinese Department. So, when we were told on arrival that there was a 'problem' with rooms—there was a shortage of them—and that the foreign students would have to share rooms with each other rather than with Chinese, Lyn and I asked whether it would be possible for us to share, as we were, after all, married. The response was typical of the China of the time. The comrade in charge sternly announced,

"Students cannot be married"

"But we are married."

"You cannot be married. Therefore, students in China cannot live together," repeated the comrade in charge of accommodation. And that was that. Well, it was until I discovered that there were actually two empty rooms in our block. I therefore tried again to argue that Lyn and I should be offered one of the rooms.

"There are no empty rooms," said the comrade in charge of accommodation, with a stony but straight face,

"There are two empty rooms," I countered.

"They are not empty. Do you not understand?"

"Not entirely, no."

"One belongs to a French student who has left China, but she is coming back."

"The other room?"

"Will be taken over."

"When?"

"Soon."

'Who by?'

"A member of the Foreign Student's Office' (in other words a snooping bureaucrat).

"When?'

"Soon."

"Next week. Tomorrow?"

"Soon."

When we left Fudan ten months later, The French student had not returned. And, although the member of the Foreign Students' Office did indeed turn up 'soon', he did not move into the free room.

So, instead of sharing a room with Lyn or with some Chinese students, I spent the first weeks at Fudan sharing with a Norwegian and K. The living quarters were segregated, with men and women housed on alternate floors. However, we did get to move in with Chinese roommates, with one foreigner and two Chinese to a room, within three weeks of arrival.

It took the Norwegian and myself just a few minutes to unpack and we then watched, speechless, and in growing amazement as K silently and methodically unpacked his aluminium trunk. First he produced a set of curtains. This in itself would have been noteworthy enough, but what was truly awe-inspiring was that they appeared to have been made to measure for the room's windows. (We later learned that they had indeed been made to measure, as K had spent some of the previous year at Fudan).

He then hung the curtains with the minimum of fuss. Next out of the trunk was a coffee pot, filters for the coffee and a large bag of roasted coffee beans. Still choosing to remain silent, he started to make a pot of coffee. Then he turned his attention back to the trunk and out came salt tablets, several packets of contraceptives (for the Fudan social round?), special light-filtering sun glasses, a large coffee cup and its companion saucer. Finally, he proceeded to unpack an extensive wardrobe of clothes, all of which seemed to have been neatly ironed.

Unpacking complete, he finally turned to us, smiled, introduced himself and offered each of us a cup of perfectly brewed coffee. K and I were to become firm friends over the course of the year.

The unpacking over, it was time to explore the campus. The first sight of it as we arrived through its forbidding main gates gave the impression of concrete drabness and walking around the campus did little to dispel that first impression. The campus was comprised of a series of square gray concrete blocks each of which housed an academic department and sleeping quarters for the that department's students. Thus, we had been delivered to the Chinese Department which also acted as the hall of residence for the Chinese Department's students. To call these gray concrete block 'departments' was something of a misnomer, as they were not departments in the usual sense. There were few lecture rooms in them, and none of the departmental staff had their offices there. In fact, I was never able to discover if our lecturers had actual offices—most had accommodation on campus and these acted as offices—or whether there was an actual Chinese Department somewhere.

Among these gray slabs stood a longer, more imposing building with a green-tiled roof with a flight of concrete steps leading up to its main entrance. These turned out to be where the lecture rooms were. Nearby was the library, another imposing building, and then the most imposing building of all, the administration block. By the main gates, as one entered the campus, stood a large statue of Mao.

On my walk back to our 'department', I noticed that a flock of Chinese students were heading towards a low stone building carrying towels and enamel wash basins. My heart sank as this suggested that the departments had no shower rooms of their own and that to have a shower would mean traipsing across the campus carrying enamel wash basins, soap, etc. This assumption proved correct.

In addition to the Chinese students heading off for the shower block, there were many others on bikes, with bells constantly ringing, as they cycled at speed across campus. I initially tried to avoid them by changing course but soon learned that this was the option most likely to lead to accidents. Instead, seasoned pedestrians learned to maintain their speed and direction. This allowed the cyclists to be able to plot your trajectory and thus, theoretically at least, avoid crashing into you.

I then walked along 'wall poster alley', where people could post their political views and criticisms of policies, people and campaigns past and present. We soon learned that these 'large character wall posters' were compulsory reading if we wanted to stay abreast of what was happening and far more informative than official publications such as the dreadful People's Daily newspaper.

The campus also boasted several basketball courts, some gardens, which appeared to have had little care for some time, a swimming pool – closed for the winter months – and, of course, a large canteen. It was with a mix of trepidation and anticipation that, clutching our enamel food bowls and tin spoons, we set off for our first culinary experience of the Fudan University canteen.

12

'WHERE ARE YOU GOING?'

On the way to the canteen clutching our bowls and spoons, every Chinese who passed us going the other way asked, "Where are you going?" This seemed an unnecessary question given that we were carrying bowls and spoons and must therefore be most likely headed for the canteen. It was only a few days later that we learned that to ask, 'Where are you going?' was a very common Shanghainese way of saying 'How are you?' and did not require a specific answer. However, even after learning this communicative style, it was often hard to resist the temptation to reply to someone who asked, 'Where are you going?' as you wandered along carrying your enamel wash basin, with a towel slung over your shoulder and carrying a pair of the special bathroom slippers in one hand, "I thought I might go to the bank and see about an opening an account." And I never really knew how to respond to the 'Where are you going?' as I made my way to the lavatory with a roll of toilet paper in my hand.

We arrived at the canteen, a huge building with a concrete floor with row upon row of wooden benches set alongside long wooden tables. There were several serving hatches, all but one of which, were attended by long queues. The serving hatch without a queue had the sign 'Western food' hanging above it. We were to discover that 'Western food' really meant pork chops and eggs, and that the queue for these would have been much longer had the Chinese students been able to afford them.

Naturally we felt that we wouldn't be seen dead queuing for Western food on our first day so we each joined one of the other queues, not knowing quite what to expect. Again, we were soon to discover that it made no difference which queue you joined, since the food served from each hatch was the same. And in the November of 1976 in Shanghai and through most of 1977, that meant a daily diet of steamed rice, which had not been properly washed as it was always replete with small stones, chewy gristly meat and limp leaves of Chinese cabbage. This diet was occasionally leavened by a soup and noodles. Breakfast brought lumps of steamed dough. The Institute's canteen had been the Savoy by comparison. Meals at the Fudan canteen were never meals to look forward to.

One of the major problems that foreign students faced in China at that time was that it was impossible for us to form any sort of personal ties or friendships with the Chinese, with the exception of those who became our roommates. Contacts with bureaucrats dominated our dealings with the Chinese. Bureaucrats are not necessarily saints in any society, but the bureaucrats we had to deal with had making sure we didn't 'stray' as their primary objective. This included ensuring we did not establish contact and possible friendships with the locals. All this under the guise of preserving our 'safety'. Our relationships with them were prickly at best, therefore. And to have been able to have a chat and share a beer and a laugh with the 'normal' Chinese would have provided a splendid remedy or antidote to bureaucracy-inspired frustrations. That remedy was simply unavailable at the time. The rules that foreigners, despite being officially referred to as 'foreign friends', were off limits were not always understood by the Chinese themselves, as the examples below show:

> An old chap approached Lyn and me in the street. He
> had a kind face creased with a smile. He appeared
> genuinely interested in learning about where we were
> from and what we were doing in China. He told us
> he used to have English friends in the Shanghai of
> the 1940s. After only a few minutes, a member of the
> dreaded security police appeared and he was ushered
> away.
>
> We went to a local restaurant. Someone came over
> to our table and asked us if we were foreign students
> studying at the university up the road. He wanted to
> know what subject we were studying. Then the boss of
> the restaurant came over and sternly ordered the man
> to leave the 'foreign friend' alone.
>
> I started chatting to a chap near the main gate of
> the university campus. He spent the next three hours
> being interrogated by members of the university
> bureaucracy.

The tragic result of this was that we felt obliged to ignore and
turn away from anyone who approached us for a chat, as we
knew that if they were seen chatting to us—and the likelihood
of that was very high as the police seemed to be everywhere—
they would be taken away for interrogation and who knows
what else. This must have made us seem aloof, uncaring and
downright rude to the locals.

One of our number thought that offering to teach English
would be a way of getting to know some local students, so
she approached the bureaucracy to make the offer to act as an
English teacher.

"Impossible!" came the immediate reply.

"But I would be happy to help and teaching would also help me understand more about China and Chinese culture," she argued, unsuccessfully.

In a society that made much of the concept of 'mutual help', her offer, unsolicited as it was, was viewed with grave suspicion. Far from learning about Chinese culture, her real motivation was no doubt to infect innocent Chinese students with evil Western ideas. And, as for meeting local students, the bureaucrat ended the conversation by solemnly pronouncing, "Foreign students have ample opportunities to talk to Chinese students during mealtimes in the canteen."

As the description of my first visit to the canteen may have intimated, it was not the sort of place that one immediately associated with being a place to strike up friendships with locals. Three minutes really isn't long enough to get to know someone. And three minutes was about as long as a Chinese student took to devour a meal. And if you are going to devour a meal of stone-riddled rice, gristly meat and limp vegetables in three minutes, the mouth has to be constantly engaged in a mixture of chewing, expelling (the stones, bones and any gristle which has proved to be indigestible) and swallowing. The Chinese tended to eat with their mouths open, so observing food being devoured and expelled in this way, was not an attractive sight. It was not easy to initiate any form of conversation at all, let alone strike up a friendship under such circumstances. Added to which the canteen itself did not really encourage lingering over coffee, and not only because there was no coffee available. Sitting on an uncomfortable wooden bench at a table strewn with the debris of meat bones, stones and chewed gristle of earlier eaters was not an experience one sought to prolong. The bureaucrat clearly felt he was pretty safe when he said there would be plenty of time for foreign students to talk to Chinese during meal times.

While the university bureaucracy as a whole had a good idea of what its task was — to prevent the foreign students getting to know any of the locals either on or off campus — there were many individual members of it who had no idea what they were doing most of the time. A prime example of personal ineptitude was provided by 'Little Wang'. This man behaved like a beheaded chicken for a great percentage of his waking hours.

Little Wang's first problem was a gross inferiority complex which, it must be said, was richly deserved. When he was seconded to the foreign student branch of the Fudan University bureaucracy, rumor had it that he had previously held a similar position, but had behaved in such an inane manner that he had been suspended from all duties and sent for a spot of re-education. It was therefore a re-educated improved model of Little Wang that was unleashed upon us. If the Mark 2 model really represented an advance on the Mark 1 version, heaven knows that the Mark 1 version had been like.

In China the epithet 'little' was used for all people who were younger than the speaker and to whom they needed not show respect. Size had no bearing on this. A person two meters tall would be referred to as 'Little X' if they happened to be younger than the speaker. It could also be a marker of friendship. Sadly, for Little Wang, however, he was not only young — in his early twenties — but he was also small, causing some to refer to him unkindly as 'Little Little Wang', a form of address that had nothing to do with friendship and one that did not bolster his already minimal self-respect.

13

LITTLE LITTLE WANG AND THE ALTERCATION AT THE HISTORY MUSEUM

Among the people that the Chinese were constantly urged to learn from was a character called Lei Feng. Lei Feng was a member of the People's Liberation Army. His every waking moment was focused on becoming the perfect communist. To this end, he devotedly and unquestioningly imbued the works of Chairman Mao. He achieved nationwide fame for working beyond and above the call of duty as he beavered away to build socialism. He was not the type to take a day or two off if he felt under the weather or had broken a finger or two. He was constantly on the lookout for opportunities to perform sterling acts of self-sacrifice. Few men can have carried so many pieces of luggage for their fellows or helped more startled old ladies across roads. He was a boy scout and one with a mission. His name was immortalized in the catchy number *Learn from Lei Feng, a Fine Model*. This blared incessantly from loudspeakers in an attempt to instill in the new breed of worker-peasant-soldier some rudimentary form of social awareness and civic duty. Unfortunately, the Party was unable to contrive a heroic martyr's death for this particular dullard. (Unlike the soldier hero, 'Bonehead Wang', who had died while saving the lives of colleagues by diving onto a hand grenade to smother the explosion, a hand grenade he himself had carelessly dropped, this being a possible explanation for his nickname being 'Bonehead'). No, poor Lei Feng was to be denied a hero's death. He died by being hit on the head by a falling telephone pole while riding in an open ox cart.

Lei Feng was Little Wang's source of inspiration. It was an unfortunate choice. Little Wang's job at the university was to 'look after' the foreign students. Sadly, there was nothing in that best-seller of the 1970s, "Lei Feng's Diary", on the subject of foreigners and how to deal with them. Little Wang's own knowledge of foreigners appeared limited. One suspects that a glimpse of a member of one of China's national minorities would have brought him up short as he realized that not everyone in the world looked as he did. But he knew what to do with people who did look different. He would put them on the path to salvation and truth by encouraging them to read the thoughts of Chairman Mao and to learn from Lei Feng. This was the approach he initially adopted with the foreign students. And when we told him to bugger off — which was frequently — he was at a loss at how to proceed. He first displayed anger, then rage. When this had no effect, he broke down in tears. In his discomfort and uncertainly, he started to fear and despise us.

He dreamed of the day when the people of China would hold him up as a hero. Perhaps a letter of recommendation from the Head of the University Revolutionary Committee, or from the Shanghai Committee or even, perhaps, from the Central Committee itself. The publication of *The Diary of Little Wang, Communist Superstar*.

He determined the way to achieve these dreams was to thwart the foreign students at every step. He became an infernal busybody, interfering on every possible occasion.

The occasion of our visit to the History Museum in Shanghai

gave free reign to Little Wang's constant need to meddle and interfere. In front of certain exhibits was a sign asking visitors not to photograph those particular exhibits. The majority of exhibits displayed no such sign. Tellingly, as it proved, the signs were written only in English and French and not Chinese, which, in itself, suggested that Chinese were not allowed to visit the museum.

Little Wang had, he told us, studied English but one could be forgiven for finding this surprising on attempting to converse with him in that language. Now, Little Wang bore a great resentment against us all, but the person for whom he felt the greatest dislike and distrust was undoubtedly K. And K had a camera.

The combination of Little Wang's inability to read the signs and K's desire to take a photo of an ancient jar gave rise to what the Chinese refer to as a 'contradiction'. As K bent forward, camera poised (and, being K, it was, of course an exceptionally fine camera) to take a photo of the jar, a mass of blurred blue filled the lens. K looked up in surprise to see Little Wang deliberately standing between the camera and the jar K wished to photograph. K made an impatient gesture to wave Little Wang out of the way. Little Wang remained where he was. K slowly uncurled himself from his stoop to his full height and towering a good foot above Little Wang, invited him, gruffly, but politely, to step aside.

"Please move, Little Little Wang."

Little Wang thought his moment had arrived. Drawing on pools of accumulated righteous wrath and anticipating the next day's headline, "Little hero defies bearded foreigner," Little Wang smirked and said, "It is forbidden to take photographs of these exhibits."

K was not impressed. "Oh do get out of the way, you silly

little man."

"It is forbidden to take photographs of these exhibits," repeated Little Wang, voice rising in volume.

K tried reasoning, pointing out that only certain of the exhibits were not to be photographed but most could be, as was the one he wanted to photograph.

"So do get out of the way, my little bureaucratic friend."

"Lies, Lies!" cried Little Wang, his voice now rising to a shout.

"It is forbidden to take photographs of these exhibits!"

By this time, everyone's attention had been drawn to the incident. The foreign students watched with a certain amusement. The other Chinese cadres and teachers from the university with embarrassment. Then, K's patience suddenly evaporated. Without saying anything, he took a step towards Little Wang, grabbed the front of his Mao jacket in his left hand and flicked him out of the way across the museum floor. He bent down again to take his photo. Little Wang, however, was made of stern stuff. Picking himself up off the floor, he came charging back, now screaming, "Stop, stop. It is forbidden to take photographs!'

Mercifully, at this point the museum curator appeared. He put his arm around Little Wang and whispered something into his ear. K clicked away. Little Wang was crushed with humiliation. He had made an idiot of himself in front of the very people he despised and distrusted. He had lost face in a big way with his colleagues. No hero he, just a stupid fool.

14

TEN DAYS LEARNING FROM THE WORKERS

The University bureaucracy, with its unerring instinct for the impractical and idiotic, decreed that a session of 'Open Door Schooling', during which we would be sent to a factory to 'learn from the workers', would take place in January. January is typically Shanghai's coldest month and the January of 1977 excelled in this regard. It was Shanghai's coldest month for thirty years.

Despite the cold — it was minus seven degrees Celsius — there was an unmistakable air of *joie de vivre* as we boarded the bus that would deliver us to the factory. Unlike our earlier experience of Open Door Schooling at Evergreen Commune in Beijing, this time we were to live at the factory for the full ten days. We were happy to be escaping the stultifying atmosphere of the classes (more on these later) and excited at the prospect of discovering what life was like for people working in a Shanghai factory. We were also happy and excited because, despite the presence of a couple of the lecturers guilty of delivering those classes and the ever-present Little Wang, we were, for the first time since our arrival in China, going to have a chance to meet locals and, what's more, to meet them in their own environment and on their own terms.

The bus set off on its journey to the northwest of the city and, before long, we were in what approximates countryside on the outskirts of Shanghai. As it was winter, we could only imagine the green fields lying under their current carpet of snow. Rows upon rows of pylons stood eerily, stretching into the distance, eventually disappearing behind the cloud of smog that hung in the air. The snow had a light grayish-yellow hue to it and looked as though it could have done with a wash.

After a while, the road withered to a narrow lane and we bumped along, passing occasional hamlets each consisting of a few single story stone-houses. Eventually we reached a little bridge that took us over a creek before coming to a stop in front of the factory gates. The sign above the gates indicated that we had arrived at Shanghai's Number 1 Machine Tool Factory. It would appear to be a somewhat wild and remote branch of the machine tool industry. And a cold one.

As Shanghai lies south of the Yangtse River, it was not, at that time, entitled to any central heating. This rule applied to all residences and factories. And for those who would wonder why a fully functioning factory would need central heating, there are two ripostes. First, as we discovered, it would be misleading to have called the Shanghai Number 1 Machine Tool Factory a fully functioning enterprise; and second, the temperature on the factory floor hovered around a brisk minus eight degrees Celsius.

It was the cold that led Little Wang to a second humiliation. We were all scheduled to start work at 7:00 a.m. None of the machine tool lathes actually started working until at least half past. The first half hour of the day was the coldest, as we stood around waiting impatiently for the 'Master Worker' lathe operators to get their machines going. Until, that is, one of the girls in our group came up with the idea of starting the day with some skipping. Showing excellent initiative, she managed to persuade one of the workers to take a break from his drive to build socialism to building a skipping rope. Thus, had you been passing the Shanghai Machine Tool Plant's Number 1 Workshop on January 13, 1977, you would have been witness to the following curious, if not to say unique, spectacle.

The Australian student who had commissioned the skipping rope arrived at work, collected the rope and started skipping. Little Wang appeared. Unable to control his insatiable desire to organize, he suggests a competition: who can make the most turns of a skipping rope within a minute of skipping?

He naturally chooses to go first. It was an impressive performance, it has to be said. He put everything he had into it and skipped feverishly for his sixty seconds. Then, face glistening with sweat and, with a swagger of anticipated triumph, he passed the rope to the second contestant.

The next few minutes saw a parade of foreign students skipping, but no one came close to threatening the total compiled by Little Wang. When everyone had skipped, we turned to Little Wang to congratulate him, but he had somehow disappeared within the last minute or so. This was surprising as Little Wang was not the sort of person to lightly forego a moment of triumph, especially over the foreign students.

A search was carried out. It ended under a machine tool lathe, for it was there that the unfortunate Little Wang had passed out, having apparently over-exerted himself in the skipping competition. A gentle slap on each cheek revived him to the extent that he opened his eyes.

"Are you all right?"

One of those absurd questions one asks when the person being addressed is clearly not 'all right'.

"Of course," replied Little Wang, an equally absurd answer, given the circumstances. Indeed, those two words were the last words he was to utter for several hours. In attempting to stand up to show that he was, "Of course, all right", he collapsed once again into a heap on the factory floor. A heap that resembled a jelly as an inadvertent twitch ran through it. We carried the unfortunate man to the factory sick bay where China's all-cure panacea was administered: an injection of glucose. He was then carried back to his bunk in the dormitory where he lay for the rest of the day.

When we returned to the dormitory after work we again inquired whether he was okay. This time there was no "of course" from the prostrate figure in the bunk. Just silence, broken by muffled sobs of shame. I was actually starting to feel sorry for the man.

The factory was bleak. Two concrete rooms were to serve as makeshift dormitories, one for the females and one for the males. Into each makeshift dormitory, a number of several steel-framed two-tier bunks had been placed. These dormitories added to the bleakness of the place. Damp concrete ceilings, damp concrete walls and damp concrete floors soon led to damp bunks, damp bedding, damp clothes and damp female and male comrades. Those among us dumbly diligent enough to do some washing during our stay were rewarded with wet and dripping smalls hanging from a clothesline in the communal shower room for the duration.

We soon had to get used to the joys of springing out of bunk at 5:30 a.m. on cold dark January mornings, struggling into layer upon layer of damp clothing at feverish speed and heading for breakfast. These living conditions – worse than those of a British public school as I can vouch from personal experience – started to take their toll. Our school bus was soon acting as an ambulance ferrying students who had succumbed and come down with severe colds back to the relative warmth of the university. I mentioned earlier that no one living south of the Yangtse was entitled to central heating. That was not strictly true as we had managed to persuade the university bureaucracy to provide heaters in our rooms. For some reason, I had been elected to be our spokesperson, and by this time we had begun to share with Chinese students, one foreigner and two Chinese to a room, a much roomier arrangement than the typical eight-bunk rooms that the Chinese students were assigned. I sought their advice on how best to make this request for heating. Should I, for example, just go in and say,

"We need heating. We are freezing to death in our rooms."

This was greeted with a look of horror on the faces of both my roommates.

"No, no, no,' they said, you must first explain the problem. So, when I found myself face to face with the 'responsible bureaucrat', the dialogue went something like this:

"Good afternoon."

"Good afternoon. How are you, student Ke?"

"Actually I am having trouble sleeping."

No reaction so I pressed on.

"I am beginning to feel unwell."

Still nothing, so on I went:

"It is so cold I cannot sleep. I shiver and shiver."

Finally, a reaction. "Are you cold? Have you caught a fever?"

"I'm freezing and feel unwell."

"Perhaps you would like some heating?"

"Oh, some heating would be wonderful. Would it be possible?"

"Perhaps, we'll see."

Thanking them profusely, I bowed my way out of the office and returned to my roommates and reported how the dialogue had gone. They professed themselves satisfied. They stressed that the technique of making requests of this nature was to get the person you were asking to be able to deduce what you were asking for. You gave all sorts of hints and reasons why you needed something and allowed them to actually voice the specific item first. This had the added advantage, within the Chinese cultural tradition, of affording the bureaucrat great face. She or he could be seen as being suffused with empathy by offering what the requestor was asking for.

As the bureaucrat had raised the question of heating before I had actually done so, my roommates felt that we would soon get heating. And, within a few days, heaters had been installed in all rooms containing foreign students.

So, those who returned early from the factory with their chills and fevers were able to benefit from recuperating in a warm room. In addition to the usual colds and fevers, there were two unusual medical cases, both involving French students. The first case involved a girl who, as the Chinese say, 'knew how to speak'. This she did loudly and continuously through most of her waking hours. Then, to the relief of many, she lost her voice. The curious thing was that it seemed to take her sometime to realize what had happened. She wandered around the factory floor as usual expressing her views on a catholic variety of subjects, except that no sounds emanated. She had suddenly become voiceless. She returned to the university.

The second case involved one of the French male students, the son of a very high-ranking French military officer. He was also extraordinarily tall. Very tall people meet several obstacles in their daily lives. They may have to have clothes or shoes specially made. Their heads are more susceptible to blows from roof beams and door lintels. They sit with backs hunched in car seats designed for the 'average' person. Their feet protrude from beneath bedclothes and dangle over the edge of their beds while trying to sleep in hotel rooms. While these are problems that are likely to be encountered by someone approaching seven feet tall anywhere in the word, they became particularly acute in China. For example, it made no difference to the number of cloth coupons a person was allocated, whether they were four foot eight inches or six foot eight inches tall. A particular hazard was that many Chinese shops at the time had a system of placing money in a heavy metal tin which was attached to a system of wires that led to the cashier's desk. These tins were then zipped back and forth along these wires. A tall person had to exercise extreme caution to avoid either being garrotted by the wires or being whacked against the side of the head by a rapidly traveling metal tin. However, it was none of the usual problems that beset the tall Frenchman. Somehow, at temperatures well below freezing, he had managed to develop a pair of grossly enlarged testicles, thereby overthrowing the conventional wisdom of the effect of cold on the nether regions of male brass monkeys. It did not take him very long to realize his affliction and he promptly returned to the university. Happily, reports had it that his testicles soon returned to normal size, about the only things about him that were.

Apart from these excitements, factory life followed a predetermined routine. Up early in the dark cold mornings and attempting to get from the bunk into clothes as swiftly as possible. Those that could face breakfast did so, others remained a precious half an hour extra in bed. But sleeping in was not easy given that the metal framed bunks creaked alarmingly whenever their occupants moved.

Breakfast over—boiled egg, rice porridge, execrable coffee— we trudged over to the workshop to which we had been seconded, showing a marked lack of enthusiasm for the hours that lay ahead. We must have made quite a sight to the locals: a bunch for foreigners wearing the factory-provided uniforms of ill-fitting blue caps, ill-fitting blue overalls and great big steel-toed boots clumping mournfully to work. The workshops were always silent at that hour as the machines themselves did not start operating until about half an hour into the shift. So the working day began with a cup of tea, a cigarette or two and, for some, some skipping.

This start to the day also gave us the chance to chat to the Chinese workers in the work team to which we had been assigned. Each of us had been put under the charge of an individual worker whose unfortunate task it was to try and educate his 'foreign trainee' in the complexities of the machine tool lathe. It was with these individuals that it was possible to lay the foundations for friendship.

My particular overlord, Foreman Shi, soon realized that he wasn't going to be able to make me into a 'master' machine tool lathe operator in the ten days we were to be at the factory. Instead he focused on finding out as much as he could about England and the English. His opening question was rather surprising,

"Can Prince Charles play football?"
"Gosh, I'm sorry, I've no idea," I replied.
This was greeted with a look of great disappointment. I had obviously lost face in not being important enough to know these things. In trying to recover some of my lost face, I then made a foolish mistake. I tried to explain that while I was not sure about the Prince's prowess on the football field,
"But he is a very good player of polo," I ventured.
Perhaps, not surprisingly, Foreman Shi's knowledge of polo appeared to be non-existent. Attempting to explain the rudiments of this sport proved tricky. It was not made any easier by my not knowing what the Chinese for horse polo was. Seeing

his confusion, I had another go at explaining it. "Horse ball," I offered.

This intelligence was greeted with such a look of baffled astonishment that I dread to think what Foreman Shi believes what the Prince does to or on horses.

The machines usually kicked into life at around a quarter to eight. A few minutes later, several would usually expire. Indeed, on a workshop floor boasting a dozen machine tool lathes, there was no occasion on any of the ten days that we were there that they were all running at the same time. To see three or four machines lying idle because of some minor fault was a common sight. A minor fault becomes serious if there is no one around to fix it. So, machines lying idle and workers idling around was the rule. My conception of a whole mass of Chinese workers painstakingly toiling away to build socialism was very swiftly shown to be yet another illusion about the way of life in China. The contrary appeared to be the case. Seldom has so little been accomplished by so many. Not only did the shifts never start on time, and not only were several lathes lying idle for extended periods of time, even those lathes which were working were not being worked very hard. The number of tea breaks held accounted for the equal number of loo breaks. The workers had thought up a legion of skives to stop their machines and sneak off for a few minutes. One popular ruse involved the sharpening of the cutting edges of the blades on the machine tool lathes. People were constantly stopping their machines to go off to sharpen their blades. And, as there were only two sharpening machines in the whole place, there was always a queue and thus a chance to chat and while away the time. And one might as well have a cup of tea and wait until the queue died down. Which, of course, it never did.

There were three major reasons for this general lack of enthusiasm for work. First, only someone who was prepared to work extremely hard would receive anything extra for so doing. And this extra took the form of one extra yuan (about thirty-five British pence at the time) a month and a nice red paper carnation of the sort appended to prize winning livestock at country shows. The second reason for taking it easy was that no one appeared to be in charge and have authority. There were workers like Foreman Shi who gloried in the name of foreman, but I never heard a foreman asking, let alone ordering, anyone to get back to work. The slogan, "The workers are the bosses", which had been promulgated by the Gang of Four, was religiously observed in the Shanghai Number 1 Machine Tool Factory.

The third, and perhaps most significant reason for the general feeling that work should not interfere too much with leisure time was that, like almost all Chinese enterprises of the time, the factory was a State-Owned Enterprise (SOE). These SOEs might have been extremely inefficient in productivity terms, but they were highly effective in providing Chinese workers and their families a living, for they were much more than a factory. Each SOE provided free on-site living quarters for the workers and their families. They also provided clinics, hospitals and educational facilities for children up to and including secondary school. There were also shops and canteens on site. Little wonder then, that a job in a SOE was considered an 'iron rice bowl', as it guaranteed lifelong employment and access to free accommodation, health care and education. What it did not guarantee was an efficient productive workforce.

The January weather did not encourage productivity either. Who wants to work when the temperature on the shop floor is minus eight degrees Celsius, with the more delicate and fiddly aspects of machine tooling and who thus found it impossible to wear gloves in the course of their work.

An atmosphere of lethargy and apathy pervaded the place,

except on one memorable occasion. The only time we saw workers pulling together as a team to produce something was when some bright spark suggested that they shouldn't waste all the snow, but use it to build a snowman. As soon as this idea went round the factory floor, machines were turned off and the entire workforce went outside to build a snowman. And a most impressive snowman it turned out to be. It stood a good two meters tall. Accessories such as hair, eyes, ears, nose and mouth were all provided by metal shavings collected from the floor of the factory. There was much laughter and banter in the making of it. It represented a grand morning's work, and one enjoyed by all. The fruits of our labor remained for the duration of our stay.

Lunch was at eleven. It was taken in the factory canteen at long wooden benches placed alongside long wooden tables. The food lacked appeal and variety. Meat was scarce in the Shanghai of the 1970s, so there was very little of that. Meals comprised some form of staple — either rice or noodles — and vegetables, almost always Chinese cabbage. What was memorable about those lunches was the Chinese factory worker who would flourish a pair of sliver chopsticks from his inside pocket. They were thinner than the average Chinese chopstick, elegantly tapered and connected at the top by a delicate silver chain. He explained that they had been handed down through the family. How he had come into their possession was not the major point of interest, however. How he had the nerve to use, and so ostentatiously, a pair of silver chopsticks in the China of 1977 was. Wooden chopsticks or tin spoons were the norm.

Lunch over, we strolled back to the workshops to work until three, time for our 'rest' and the end of our shift. Then the next shift took over and they worked until 10:00 p.m. The factory would then close for the night. The reason why the factory only ran two shifts was that it was simply too cold to run a night shift.

The afternoon monotony of tea breaks, machine breakdowns and blade sharpening was interrupted twice a week by an hour-long political study session. Each workshop team, consisting of about a dozen people, and now including one foreign student, would find a convenient spot to gather. The team's political leader – almost inevitably a member of the CCP and, in all likelihood the only member of the CCP in the team – would try and lead what he hoped would be a political discussion.

At that time, all China was supposed to be ardently and enthusiastically studying an article penned by Mao in the 1950s entitled "On the Ten Great Relationships." Whatever you may think of the importance of the thoughts of Mao, most would agree his is not a snappy writing style. The famous *Little Red Book* was produced in order to get across his message in language accessible to the masses. "On the Ten Great Relationships," on the other hand, is not the easiest political tract to read. The four of us who had studied Chinese at Leeds had a bit of a march on the others, as we had studied the article as part of our course in Chinese political documents.

Everyone in our group had earlier been given a copy of the article so we could prepare for these political study meetings. Needless to say, two or three people always contrived to forget to bring their copies of the article to these meetings. Needless to say, it was always the same two or three.

Once the group was sitting in a circle and had settled, the political leader would call the meeting to order and ask us to open the article at the page we had got to at the previous meeting. This was the well-tried 'Please open your books at page XX' ploy. He would then begin the discussion by saying something along the lines of, "Well, I'm sure you all remember where we got to last time," whereupon the class would shuffle uncomfortably, with its collective gaze fixed resolutely at some point on the floor in front of them. A couple of apologetic giggles would emanate from the group, as if to confess that what they had studied last time might not have really sunk in.

The political leader would glance censoriously at the gigglers before setting the ball rolling by asking someone to read the first paragraph of the day's text.

"Comrade Hu, please read from where we left off last time."

Comrade Hu remained silent.

"Comrade Li, perhaps you could read for us."

Comrade Li remained silent.

The whole performance would have been absurd — a group of factory workers interrupting their work to read paragraph by paragraph an article written by Mao. It would have been absurd had it not been embarrassingly pitiful. It was pitiful as very few of the workers in the group could read with any fluency and several could not read at all. The poor person who had been nominated would remain silent or struggle over the first sentence they had been asked to read. The political leader would then become impatient, interrupt the struggler and nominate someone else to take over, and the pattern would be repeated. It was excruciatingly embarrassing for the foreign students when it transpired that they were the only people, other than the political leader, who were able to read the Chinese with any fluency.

In the end, our political leader would give up and simply read the article aloud and then explain to them what Mao was trying to say. This potentially gave him great power, as they were completely dependent upon him to tell them what an article said and what it meant. After the day's set text had been read and explained, the political leader would ask for questions. Once again, eyes would become downcast and the occasional giggle heard. Although I only attended four of these sessions at my time in the factory, and it may, of course, have been my presence that caused the reticence, but not once did anyone ask a single question. The political 'discussion' soon descended into a general chat; members of the group moved off for tea, mugs cupped in both hands for warmth, and that day's political discussion session would come to an ill-defined end.

Not all the foreign students at the factory were engaged in working on the factory floor. For example, Lyn managed to secure an extremely cushy billet. She spent the day dressed in a white coat, a garment that added instant prestige to the wearer, as it signaled some form of indoor or office work. In her case, she assembled transistors. It was not hard work. The transistor assembly group somehow managed to reach their monthly quota by the tenth day of each month. For the remainder of the month, they passed their time playing games. One such involved trying to count to a hundred without making a mistake in the shortest possible time. According to Lyn, this occasioned hours of innocent amusement in the transistor radio division. I wondered whether their apparent inability to count might not have seen them miscalculate the number of transistors they assembled, explaining why they always seem to meet their quota so early.

That the Transistor Assembly Division managed to get away with doing even less work than the rest of the factory did not go unnoticed by the lathe operators. When I told Foreman Shi that my wife was working assembling transistors and went to work each day wearing a nice white coat he was abruptly dismissive.

"Too easy," he snorted, "Anyone could do that work."

With our shift ending at 3:00 p.m., we had considerable time in which to try and amuse ourselves. There was, however, little provision for extra-curricular activity at the factory. Had we been at the factory at a different time of the year, rather than in the midst of one of Shanghai's coldest winters in memory, we would have been able to explore the surrounding countryside.

But no doubt, the bureaucracy would not have been happy at the thought of foreign students prowling around, untended, the neighborhood. As we were practically snowed in, it was not a problem they had to face.

In the event, the time between the end of the shift and bed was divided up into three main activities: showers, supper and ping-pong. Of the three, it was, without doubt, the shower that gave the most pleasure. The water was blessedly hot. Under the shower was the only time we could feel warm, and the inner-warmth it also generated lasted for about three quarters of an hour before the bone-chilling cold crept back. Under the shower, we momentarily re-discovered some *joie de vivre*. This brought forth spontaneous laughs of joy, often verging on the hysterical. This response was not shared by the locals who simply showered in a workmanlike manner. An observer, if they had been able to see through the mist and steam in the shower block, might have wondered why the gales of laughter appeared to be emanating only from foreigners. It was because we were deliciously warm again, if only for a short time.

After showers, it was time for supper. The post-shower light-headedness soon dissipated. It was difficult to get enthusiastic at the prospect of sitting down to meals that would come close to winning any 'worst in show' rosettes. It consisted of Chinese cabbage boiled almost to a pulp; occasionally there was a piece of chewy meat, the color of which was somewhere between mud and jaundice. We were informed this was pork, but none of us ever dared asked which part of the pig could produce meat of such a color and texture. All this washed down by soup for which the adjective insipid could have been especially created.

Supper over, it was time for activity number three: ping-pong. We didn't play ping-pong for the fun of it as much as for keeping warm. Unfortunately, there was only one table, so the ping-pong room was full of people huddled around the walls, wrapped up in thick winter overcoats, patiently waiting their turn to play and get warm.

And that was about it: showers, supper and ping-pong. It was not even possible to fend off the cold with a warming tot or two of the local firewater. The factory store, such as it was, sold no alcohol. And, in my view, if ever there had been a store that needed to sell alcohol, the Shanghai Number 1 Machine Tool factory store was it. Fortunately, I had foreseen this possible eventuality and had brought along some supplies of the deadly white spirit or *bai jiu*. One of the Swiss students had brought along some excellent coffee so we teamed up in the evenings to consume what we called 'Shanghai Coffee'. Bloody good it was, too.

Had someone told us before our departure from the factory that those of us who had stayed healthy and lasted the ten-day stay at the factory and avoided being carted back to the university suffering from a range of ailments, some bizarre, would be most eager to return to the university, we would have been surprised. As it was, however, the alacrity with which we boarded the bus to return to what we now realized was the relative luxury of university life suggested we were looking forward to our return. Had we learned much from the workers on this stint on Open Door Schooling? Yes, we had learned a great deal about what life was like in a Shanghai factory. We had also struck up friendships with some of the workers. Despite my ineptitude at operating the lathe, by the time we departed, Foreman Shi had been kind enough to christen me 'Master Worker Ke.' I suspect there might have been a smidgeon of irony behind this. Sadly, however, we were informed by the bureaucracy that we would not be allowed to continue to communicate in any way with people from the factory. 'Foreign friends' could apparently learn from the workers, but never befriend them.

15

HOW ARE YOUR STUDIES GOING?

Classes in Modern Chinese Literature at Fudan were neither intellectually strenuous nor stimulating. The most difficult part of the course was managing to get to the lectures on time. It came as something of a shock to learn that classes would start at 7:30 a.m. each morning. In those days 7:30 a.m. was a time that tended to pass me by as I slept. My feeling was that, while 7:30 a.m. was an inevitable part of every day, there was no need to be awake to see it. The blow caused by the early start was, however, softened by the discovery that lectures ended at 9:10 a.m. A day's classes over before I would normally have risen. To be given a feeling of accomplishment by 9:10 a.m. was a new and gratifying experience for a person who normally only started to make much sense of things around lunchtime.

The sense of accomplishment was physical rather than mental. Classes took the form of lectures. The syllabus for the Modern Literature course was about as full as dear old Lei Feng's brain on a good day. There were only two items on it: the works of the essayist and short story writer, Lu Xun and the poetry of Mao himself. A couple of other ideas of authors who might be included floated around — the works of the propagandist Guo Moruo, for example — but these never took root.

There were two main reasons for this sparse syllabus. First, a large number of contemporary Chinese authors had been criticized over the past few years, some before the Cultural Revolution, many more during and after it. This meant that well-known modern Chinese writers, such as Ding Ling, Lao She, Ba Jin, Mao Dun and Shen Congwen, whom we had studied at university, were off the syllabus. Anyone who even mentioned their names was considered a counter-revolutionary.

Naturally, this policy robbed the course of both content and interest. It also meant that the Chinese students in the Modern Literature course were completely ignorant of these writers and their writing. This gave rise to the bizarre but embarrassing situation whereby the foreign students knew a great deal more about modern Chinese literature than their Chinese roommates. It was as if Chinese students of Modern English Literature at a British university found that, not only were their English classmates not allowed to read Graham Greene, Virginia Wolf or George Orwell, but that they had not even heard of them.

The second reason for the bare syllabus was, paradoxically, the overthrow of the very people who had been responsible for the banning of all these authors in the first place, the Gang of Four. The demise of these self-appointed guardians of Chinese culture, far from causing a tidal wave of liberalization, had, at the outset, the opposite effect. People were aware that the policies enforced by the Gang of Four were now to be eschewed. What they did not know was what policies should replace these, as there had been no official pronouncements of a new Party line. The result was a political and cultural vacuum. The safest course was, to steal a phrase from Daoism, to do nothing.

Our literary diet, therefore, resembled the grated carrot portion of health farm fare. The only two people that the authorities felt could be taught with any confidence were Lu Xun and the poems of Mao. It was, in a way fortunate, that Lu Xun had died in 1936. He had never been a member of the CCP and was far too individualist a person to have worked comfortably under a CCP regime. Had he not died when he did, it is likely he would have soon found himself labeled as a counter-revolutionary and his works banned.

Those in charge of designing the Modern Chinese Literature syllabus now found themselves in a predicament. In the previous year, the foreign students had complained that there was too much Lu Xun in the course, as they had studied only his work for three months. As a result, the authorities had, much to people's pleasant surprise, agreed to cut down on the amount of time spent studying him for the following year's course. Now, however, in the words of the syllabus designers, "There were, perhaps, problems." For, far from reducing the amount of time spent on the study of Lu Xun, they had no option but to increase it. Instead of a sole diet of Lu Xun for three months, we were destined to get two full semesters of him. This might not have been so bad, had we actually studied his writing. Instead we got two semesters of the lecturer standing in front of the class, informing us in as many ways as possible that Lu Xun was a great revolutionary thinker. There was little attempt to study the man's style or his writing. All we got was spiel upon spiel of the man's revolutionary fervor. The only people who took any serious notice of the lectures were the two or three other lecturers who 'happened' to sit in on the classes. Rather than just taking notes, they attempted to note down everything the lecturer said. They were clearly there to make sure the lecturer said nothing controversial or counter-revolutionary. Needless to say, the lecturer said nothing controversial or counter-revolutionary and restricted himself to anodyne comments and propaganda.

Anyone who might have thought that the literature lectures

lacked insight and a little zip had only to attend one of the political lectures to realize how boring a lecture could really be. These were held once a week and also delivered at 7:30 a.m. in the morning, but few people, by attending them, missed out on sleep. The politics lecturer had clearly mastered the art of political survival. His technique was, when having to speak in public, such as giving a lecture, to speak in a dialect and with an accent that no one would be likely to understand. Yet, he seemed firm in his convictions. Occasionally he would march to the blackboard and write 'Mao' or 'Revolution' or 'Liberation' or 'Gang of Four' on it alongside a number of meaningless decontextualized percentages and figures (for example, 28.6 percent, 30,000) as he continued spouting incomprehensibly. He never made eye contact with any member of his audience, which comprised a rapidly diminishing number. As attendance at these lectures became poor, the lecturer implemented a range of strategies in an attempt to bolster it. First he put the class back by half an hour to 8:00 a.m. Still nobody went. He then took to knocking on the door of our rooms in the early morning, to remind us he would soon be starting his lecture. Still nobody went, but he learned a few choice epithets in a range of European languages. In a last desperate bid to inveigle us into attending his classes, he started to give his lectures in the hall of residence itself. This ploy worked on the first couple of occasions. Being initially unaware of this new stratagem, and having no idea that the politics lectures were now being given in what was grandly called the 'magazine room', some poor fish who thought they would leaf through the latest edition of *China Reconstructs* found themselves being waylaid by a pitifully grateful lecturer, plonked in a chair and forced to endure ninety minutes' worth of incomprehensible propaganda. The unfortunates who found themselves thus ensnared could at least amuse themselves by studying the way he gave his lectures.

As he spoke, he would look up as though addressing some imaginary dress circle, unfocused eyes ablaze with revolutionary fervor, as he presumably made telling revolutionary point after telling revolutionary point. Whatever beliefs he was imparting, we had to admit that he certainly seemed to believe in them himself. I often wondered why he was so keen to get us to attend his lectures, for once he started he appeared to be oblivious of his audience. It was very much an 'Onward Maoist Soldiers' type of performance. That no one understood a word he was saying either did not occur to him or did not trouble him. Perhaps he was a little mad.

The other lecturers were anything but mad. There was the jovial 'Teacher Li' — the lecturer in Chinese Classical Literature who had come to collects us from Beijing. He was a nice fellow who was genuinely interested in his subject and his students. It became a regular sight to see him walking up and down the corridors of the Department, in discussion with one of his students. These discussions were often punctuated by shouts of laughter. He was the only lecturer or bureaucrat who, on being asked an awkward question, did not resort to the usual standard phrases of "We know these things, you can't" or, "You foreign students do not fully understand the situation in our country."

'Teacher Wu', our lecturer in Modern Chinese Literature, frequently ended discussions with remarks of this type. Any student who questioned Lu Xun's unswerving loyalty to Mao and the CCP was rebuffed with these 'You can't know these things' remarks. And, as all the facts indicated that Lu Xun would never have accepted the Party lines of the 1950s and 1960s, and, as he never even became a member of the Party during his lifetime, it was more than irritating to be told that these were things we couldn't know or understand. This is not to say that Teacher Wu was stupid. Far from it, he was extremely intelligent, but a person whose intelligence had a cunning streak that allowed him to avoid controversy and dangerous ideas. This was a shame for, on the few occasions that he would allow himself to relax, he could be both entertaining and stimulating. I remember him getting very excited when explaining the relationship between Cubism and stereophonic sound. He was sitting on one of the beds in our room trying to convince me and my Chinese roommates of the "obvious" connection between the two (a connection I have sadly since forgotten) while cigarette after cigarette got smoked down to knuckle-scorching length before being crushed into a tin ashtray overflowing with stubs.

Although the majority of our lectures were open only to foreign students – the Chinese had their own separate classes, but what they studied or learned in these was impossible to fathom – we were occasionally invited to attend mass lectures along with the Chinese students. On one such occasion a large audience assembled in Fudan's largest lecture theater to hear one of Fudan's most celebrated professors, Liu Dajie, give a talk about the famous 18th Century Chinese novel, *Hong Lou Meng*, the title of which has been variously translated as *The Dream of the Red Chamber* or as *The Story of the Stone*. This was one of the revered novels of Imperial China which had been written in the accessible vernacular language – rather than the literary language, which was known only by the highly educated elite. I was particularly looking forward to the talk as we had studied the novel at Leeds and I had developed the irreverent theory that, wherever you opened the novel, one of the main characters, the pampered and delicate heir to an extremely wealthy family, Jia Baoyu, would be in tears. The novel is a novel of manners and was praised by, among many others, Lu Xun, as offering a realistic portrayal of everyday life in wealthy Chinese households.

Excited and expectant murmurings common at such times

could be heard as we anticipated the arrival of Professor Liu. As he entered the auditorium, a hush descended as he took his place behind the lectern. And began to speak.

I suppose he had been speaking for a couple of minutes when I realized that I was not able to understand much of what was being said. I was finding it very hard to decipher his accent. I therefore turned to the Chinese student sitting next to me to ask for help. But she too confessed to having trouble understanding his accent. So I, along, I suspect, with several others sat through the Great Man's lecture feeling very much like one of the swine before which pearls were being cast.

I later wondered whether teacher Wu had managed to glean a great deal from the lecture, as he only gave us a remarkably short summary of it in class the following day. Perhaps he felt that a famous professor earning the princely sum of three hundred eighty yuan per month shouldn't be dependent upon a mere lecturer earning a meagre eighty yuan a month to translate his lectures for him.

I was talking to my two roommates about Professor Liu's lecture — they too had had difficulty following it — when the Swiss student, J, wandered into our room. He was carrying a Swiss Air calendar that he intended to give one of my roommates, who was his regular chess partner. J had also clearly decided that it was about time that his chess partner learned something about Switzerland. He proudly held up the calendar and, starting with January and a splendid Alpine snow scene, slowly turned over each month and its seasonal photograph of the Swiss countryside, pointing out aspects that he felt would be of interest. The roommates' reaction to this was certainly interesting. They had very little knowledge of the outside world and, in this, they were no different from the majority of their fellow students. They had little knowledge of the outside world simply because little knowledge of the outside world was available to them. I was surprised, therefore, and J somewhat put out, when neither roommate showed the slightest interest in any of the photos of the spectacular Swiss landscape. Only one picture captured their intention. This was not a picturesque mountain or lake scene, but one of enormous trucks and bulldozers. They studied this picture closely, all the while muttering expressions such as "Wow, so formidable, so strong."

At this, J looked scornfully at them both, and, muttering something about the parochialism of the Chinese, stomped off out of the room. With him gone, my roommates, rather than looking through the stunning scenery as portrayed in the calendar's photographs, using scissors, cut out the photos, with each roommate receiving six. They had obviously decided they did not need a pretty pictorial calendar. My initial shock that they were cutting up the calendar slowly gave way to understanding as I realized they were going to use the pictures to cover their books — all Chinese covered their books to prevent people from seeing what they were reading. But they did not cover the books with the picture side up but with it down. J's Swiss Air calendar had, in a matter of minutes, become white covering paper for a dozen books.

16

To Shaoxing: Lu Xun, wine, an opera
AND A PERFORMANCE

The Modern Literature course went some way to redeeming itself when we learned the routine of lectures was to be interrupted by a field trip. We were going to spend three days at Lu Xun's home village, Shaoxing, in neighboring Zhejiang Province. While Shaoxing is known as Lu Xun's birthplace, it is probably better known as the birth place of Shaoxing wine, a most palatable sherry-like concoction usually drunk warm out of small ceramic cups which rest snuggly in individual ceramic holders into which hot water has been poured to keep the wine warm.

Shaoxing is not far from Shanghai and we arrived in time for lunch, which was disappointingly similar to a Fudan lunch. Lunch was taking us a little longer to consume at this time as there had been a hepatitis scare and we were each given pill boxes replete with pills that we were to take three times a day with meals. I say the pill boxes were replete with pills, as we were to take thirty-three tiny little pills twice and day and thirty-four once a day. Painstakingly counting out thirty-three tiny pills takes some time. No one was able to explain why we had to take one hundred tiny pills a day as opposed to three slightly larger ones. Pills counted and consumed, we rattled off to visit the Lu

Xun Memorial House, which was actually the primary school where he had been a student. The curator reverently showed us items such as the wooden school desk at which he had studied (no names carved into the lid). The school was a pleasant building, with wooden floors and walls in an attractive setting. It was separated from the road by a narrow twisting canal and reached over a narrow bannistered footbridge. Having studied the vegetable and mineral aspects of the Memorial House, we were then introduced to the animal in the streaky thin form of a person who, it was claimed, was the grandson of a character in one of Lu Xun's short stories. He took over the guided tour but told us nothing about his grandfather and his relationship with Lu Xun. Instead, we were treated to the usual guff about how much better life was now for him and his family. "Before the liberation…" etc., etc. These questionable claims were followed by snippets of gossip about Lu Xun himself. For example, how for three years, he had had to travel long distances to procure medicines for his ailing father. How he had had to transfer to school in Nanjing, as schooling there was free. How he had arrived at school in Nanjing with only eight yuan in his pocket. And, perhaps the most absurd claim of all, how he had had to eat chillies during the winter months to keep warm.

The following morning, we were taken a few miles from Shaoxing to look around a commune named Red Mountain Commune. Quite why we were taken to this commune I'm still not sure. The organizers assured us that Lu Xun had 'quite often' visited a place, unnamed, but said to be four miles from the commune. However, the weather was splendid, a cold blue-skied crystal clear day and we all felt an exhilarating sense of freedom as we were allowed to wander, free of official chaperones, around the commune, along raised paths through fields and among groups of houses. We did notice what looked like telephone numbers scrawled on the walls of several buildings. These seemed to be advertising a range of services from bicycle repairs to feminine company.

After wandering around for a while, a few of us were surprisingly invited into a house by its clearly proud occupant. We were shown round a newly built three bed-roomed brick building in which nine people lived. We had only been in the house for a couple of minutes before we were rounded up— so much for the apparent absence of official chaperones—and taken off for the inevitable 'Simple Introduction to Life on the Commune', starting with 'Before liberation ...' etc., etc.

The simple introduction was mercifully short and we were soon back on the bus. Our disappointment at leaving the commune so early was tempered by the knowledge we were off to visit a Shaoxing distillery where the distinctive wine of the region, Shaoxing or Yellow wine, a concoction of rice, water and wheat-based yeast, was brewed. This proved well worth the visit. Walking among ranks of huge stone jars of bubbling liquid which gave off a heady, musty smell. Meeting people who were keen and happy to talk about their work rather than how their lives had so much improved since liberation. We learned that there were four types of Shaoxing: *Yang Hong, Jia Fan, Shan Niang* and *Xiang Xue*.

"Would you like to sample each of the four types and determine your preferences?"

We would indeed! I found the *Yang Hong* a little rough. Not unlike a cooking sherry with a bit of oomph. This actually forms the base of the other three wines, and is seldom drunk on its own, but typically used in cooking. The *Shan Niang* was definitely smoother and slid easily down but was a little too sweet for my taste. Then the *Jia Fan*. Ah, this was the one—not so sweet and a suggestion of power. The name literally means 'added rice' and I was told that this increased the alcohol content. Finally, the *Xiang Xue* — too sickly sweet for me. The visit confirmed me as a *Jia Fan* man and I proceeded to drink too much of it over supper that evening.

After supper, we were treated to a performance by the Shaoxing Opera group. In the past, this form of singing and opera was very ad hoc-ish. A song might last two minutes or twenty, depending on the mood of the singer and presumably that of the audience. These days, however, the form is fixed. Not being a fan of Beijing Opera — which sounds like people screeching in despair to me — or the drum-beating cymbal clashing cacophony of the Cantonese Opera of the South, I was pleasantly surprised to find the opera tuneful and melodic. Members of the audience were gaily singing along with what appeared to be local folk songs. It was also encouraging to hear that the troupe toured the local area giving performances, thus helping maintain the tradition of Shaoxing Opera. All in all, it had been a fine day, perhaps the best day of our stay in China to date.

On the third day of our visit to Lu Xun's hometown, we were taken, again for reasons I still do not know, to hear a number of elderly women talk about their lot, pre- and post-liberation. Their stories could be summarized by saying that they had had a dreadful time before liberation but their lives had steadily improved since. This would not do justice, however, to the way these stories were wrung and strung out. As the women told their tales, they became more and more hysterical as they detailed the dreadful things that had happened to them. Their performance — for that was what it surely was — became more and more grotesque as the women wailed with confected grief. Suddenly I found the whole thing hugely funny and started to giggle like a mischievous schoolboy and was soon crying along with the women, but with tears of laughter. I hoped my tears and my shaking body would be taken as evidence of empathetic sobbing rather than an attempt to conceal a serious fit of the giggles.

After the women had wailed themselves out and been led off, we were taken to visit a porcelain factory. Actually, as time was short, we were only treated to the 'Short Introduction'. This followed the drearily familiar pattern but with different information. We were told, for example, that before liberation, the factory had only produced three patterns of porcelain tableware but now produced seventeen. As we were also told that the factory had been built in response to Mao's call for 'Self Reliance', it wasn't clear how it could have made any porcelain at all before liberation, and thus before it had been built. We were also told that, before liberation, the people of Shaoxing had had to drink their wine out of cups imported from Jiangsu Province, each of which cost the equivalent of three kilos of rice to buy. Now, of course, their porcelain cups were priced so that the ordinary person could buy them. I did start to wonder whether the authors of these 'Short Introductions' might not find lucrative careers in the copyrighting or advertising business.

So ended our three-day trip to Lu Xun's birthplace. We had not learned very much about Lu Xun that we did not already know, but we had learned a lot about Shaoxing, its opera and its wine. I was able to add a coda to Teacher Wu's interpretation of Lu Xun, which was, of course, that he was a great revolutionary writer. And Shaoxing *Jia Fan* was a great revolutionary wine.

17

'FRIENDSHIP FIRST, COMPETITION SECOND'

One the way of broadening my China horizons and making some Chinese acquaintances or, hopes, friends, was, I innocently thought, to take up a sport. Few of the few foreign students at Fudan played any sport, so it would mean playing in a team with Chinese. And, as we all believe, playing a team sport builds team spirit and a sense of camaraderie. Having decided to take up a sport, the next question was, which one to choose. Several could be crossed off the list as no one played them. The choice was between basketball, volleyball, swimming, ping pong and football. I am not the right size for basketball and have never played volleyball in my life so dismissed these as options. As it was winter, the pool was closed. But my first visit to the Fudan swimming pool when it did open helped me reach a decision about making swimming a regular option. The pool was some twenty-five yards long and fifteen wide. On the side at half way stood a chair that looked as if it might have seen service decades earlier as an umpire's chair at an outside tennis court. In it sat a man, the lifesaver, who, it soon became apparent, saw his role in life not so much as saving lives but making them miserable. He spent his entire time shouting at people, both in an out of the pool, ordering them not to do what they were doing.

On my first visit, I got changed and dived in to start swimming a peaceful length of the pool. I soon discovered that swimming lengths of the pool was not allowed. I was about half way down my first (and last) length when I became aware of a voice that was displaying a remarkable range of pitch. I did not realize at the time that this voice was directed at me. I swam on, unperturbed. Approaching the end of the pool, I could still hear this voice increasing in volume. So I took my head out of the water and looked back at the 'umpire's' chair. He was standing half out of his seat in a paroxysm of hysteria, causing his rickety chair to wobble alarmingly. His arms were flailing like some epileptic boxer's and his empurpled face was staring directly at me.

"You are not allowed to swim lengths in this pool," he screamed at me.

"Me?" I pointed at myself while treading water.

"You, you foreign overseas student, you are not allowed to swim lengths in this pool!"

As I was clearly the only foreign student in the pool, it was difficult to pretend he was not addressing me.

"You are not allowed to swim in that direction in this pool!" he bellowed once more.

At this point his screaming caught up with him and he began to cough violently. For one thrilling moment I thought he might actually topple out of his chair and into the pool, but, disappointingly, he managed to remain perched in his high chair. I clambered out of the pool and wandered round to have a word with the lifesaver. By the time I arrived he had calmed down enough to explain the rules relatively coherently.

"In this pool, you are only allowed to swim widths and in one direction," he expounded.

"When you have completed a width and if you want to swim

another one (if you want to swim another one!), you must get out of the pool, walk around the edge of the pool and re-enter the pool where you started."

"Why?"

"To avoid accidents"

It was while I was standing by the lifesaver's chair pondering over what sort of accidents might occur if people were allowed to swim lengths rather than widths, when K, the German student strolled casually into the pool area. The lifesaver's eyes glinted in anticipation. This was not entirely surprising as K looked a natural transgressor. He was wearing sunglasses, with an imperial purple towel slung nonchalantly over his shoulder and a copy of the *Frankfurter Allgemeiner* (where on earth had he procured that?) under his arm. He looked, for all the world, like a man looking for a quiet place to sunbathe.

Rules were being broken. Our lifesaver sprang into immediate action.

"You must not bring swimming towels into the pool area. You must not wear sunglasses in the pool area."

K blithely ignored him and walked on at his leisurely pace.

"You," the pitch rising once more, "You foreign student must not bring a towel into the pool area!"

K continued to completely ignore him, not even turning his head to look at him.

"You", he was nearly out of his chair again now, "Must not bring a towel into the pool area," he screamed.

At this, K turned slowly towards him, pushed his sunglasses down to the tip of his nose and peered over them to look at the lifesaver.

"Me?" he innocently inquired, pointing at himself.

"Yes, you, you, you!"

At this point K slowly strolled over to the man, pointed

directly at him and told him what he thought of his swimming pool and where he could stick it. With that, he walked leisurely back out of the pool area.

Swimming therefore never provided an attractive option, even in the heat of the summer. This left ping pong and football. I did some research and went to watch local students playing ping pong. They were extraordinarily skilful. I soon realized that the chances of my making a Fudan ping pong team hovered between zero and negligible. This left football.

My first move was to ask around the Chinese Department whether anyone there played football for Fudan, or at least knew whom to approach. I was in luck as I soon discovered a second-year student who played full back for the Fudan first X1. He told me I should turn up at training, which was held at 5:00 p.m. every Tuesday afternoon. I passed this information on to the other foreign students but only K and I turned up at the next training session.

Training involved playing seven or eight a side and, needless to say, playing across the pitch widthways. Perhaps alarmingly for that year's Fudan football team's prospects, after a single training session coach Wang invited both K and me to a pre-match briefing the day before Fudan's next fixture. The briefing session was held in a small room above what Fudan referred to as the gym but was, in effect, a room with an uncovered concrete floor upon which half a dozen rickety ping-pong tables stood.

The briefing session started with Coach Wang reminding the team they had lost their previous fixture 3-0. He then asked whether any of the team could offer a possible explanation for the defeat. The response to this recalled the political study sessions at the machine tool factory. People shuffled their feet and made sure they did not make eye contact with Coach Wang. There was a long pause and it was not a pregnant one. Then, with a look of despair, Coach Wang professed his views on the subject. He gabbled on for about ten minutes aided by a piece of scratchy chalk and a blackboard that had so many cracks that it looked like a slab of crazy paving. The gist of his remarks, as far as I could follow them, was that we were unlikely to win a game of football unless we stopped giving the ball to the opposition rather than passing it to members of our own team. This was accompanied by the sound of the chalk screeching over the blackboard and its cracks as the Coach drew arrows from players marked with an X to other players marked with an X, giving advice on where the ball should be passed.

Talk of tactics over, the Coach turned to discuss the upcoming match. Fudan had a home game against the Chemical Institute. Coach Wang indicated that they should provide relatively easy opposition, but sounded a word of caution: the Chemical Institute had an Albanian center half who was big, rough and, unfortunately, a rather good footballer. I was then expecting Coach Wang to detail ways we would deal with this behemoth of a center half. Perhaps he would detail one of us to stick with him throughout the game or advise our wingers not to waste their time by centering high balls into the opposition penalty area, as the Albanian would be able to deal with these easily. However, no further tactics were discussed. Instead, he reminded the team of the then overriding slogan for all sport in China.

"Don't forget," he said, "Friendship First, Competition Second."

As we were walking back to the Chinese department, I asked our left back whether he could tell me the names of the other players. At the beginning of the briefing session, Coach Wang had introduced K and me to the other players, but had not introduced them to us. He looked surprised at being asked the question, but not half as surprised I must have looked at his reply.

"I don't know any of their names," he said.

"You don't know their names?" I repeated incredulously. After a short pause I asked,

"Well which one's the captain?"

"Oh him" he said pointing to the disappearing shape of a chap walking off into the darkness.

"And what's his name?"

"As I said, I don't know any of their names," he calmly replied, as though not knowing your team captain's name was the most natural thing in the world."

I initially assumed my Chinese Department colleague was atypical, in not knowing the names of his captain and teammates, but soon discovered this was the norm, not the exception. Not one member of the team knew the names of their teammates.

The day of the match against the Chemical Institute dawned — both K and I must have impressed at the single training session we had at that stage attended — as both of us were selected in the starting XI, K playing a defensive role and my role being to attack down the left. I proudly donned my Fudan shirt with the number seven on the back. In fact, I still have it stored safely away. I was nervous — would the foreigner make a fool of himself — and, at the same time, I was curious to see how the slogan of 'Friendship First, Competition Second' would translate onto the field of play. Would the Chinese equivalents of 'What rotten luck!' or 'Splendid play' or 'No, here you are, you have it' echo round the ground? Or would there be the normal epithets and swear words and instances of foul play?

The match started innocently enough and the reason we found ourselves two goals down after only ten minutes had more to do with our incompetence than overly gentlemanly conduct. They scored a pretty good goal early on, courtesy of a fine header by their Albanian center half. But we might have been only one goal down after the first ten minutes had our goalkeeper taken the elementary precaution of standing either on his goal line or in front of it rather than behind it. As it was, he was clearly behind his own goal line when collecting what should have been an innocuous back pass from our left back. 0-2.

Play was held up after the second goal, but the cause of the hold-up had nothing to do with ungentlemanly conduct. Quite the contrary, in fact. Our behavior was exemplary as we waited patiently and silently while watching an elderly lady wheel her bicycle diagonally across the pitch. She had a unique wheeling action. She plodded painfully slowly across the pitch, eyes fixed firmly on the ground in front of the front wheel and apparently completely oblivious to the fact that a game of football was being played — or had been — until she started crossing the pitch. The sight of that old lady, half pushing and half leaning against her bicycle as if for support, while her shopping, which included a mud fish of about one foot in length and of an extremely unsavory appearance, swaying rhythmically from the handlebars, will live long in my memory.

The diversion over, the game restarted. I soon discovered that elderly women wheeling bicycles across the pitch was not the only local hazard we had to contend with. Another hazard stemmed from the crowd's (and there was a crowd of at least a hundred) apparent ignorance of the function of touchlines. This added a unique dimension to wing play. A winger would scamper down the wing with the ball at his feet when he would simply disappear into the throng of spectators who had encroached several feet onto the pitch. Neither the opposition nor the referee had any idea where he was and whether he was still in the field of play. The winger would suddenly pop out from among this eager throng at a place of his choosing, scamper a few more paces down his wing before slicing his cross into some distant ditch behind the goal line.

We turned around at half time, three nil down. I would not have missed the third goal that was scored against us well, for all the tea in China. The use of the passive here is deliberate. As with the second goal, the third goal was not scored by the opposition. We scored it. What happened was this. There was a very strong wind blowing that day and we were playing into the teeth of it. This had already caused our defense some moments of discomfort. They appear to have read in some coaching manual that the way to get distance on a kick is to give it plenty of air. This is good advice on a calm day. It is not such good advice when you are playing into a strong wind. Several desperate clearance kicks from our defense had consequently been blown sideways into touch and, in one case, out for a corner.

I have seen some memorable own goals in my time. Our center half at school knocking the ball back towards his own gaol to give our goalkeeper an early feel of the ball, only to realize too late that the goalkeeper was still on the sidelines doing up his laces. In much more exalted circles, when playing their arch rivals, Liverpool, the Leeds United goalkeeper Gary Sprake managed the extraordinary feat of throwing the ball into his own net rather than to one of his players, when the ball somehow got stuck to one of his gloves. But neither of these own goals were executed with quite the mind-numbing incompetence as the goal that saw the Chemical Institute increase their lead to three goals.

Our goalkeeper, who had already been somewhat at fault for the second goal somehow contrived to score a goal against himself. To be fair, he had no chance of saving it. This would have required the speed of a gazelle, the athleticism of a gibbon and some common sense, attributes in which our man was lacking.

There seemed little likelihood that we would be three goals

down at half time when our goalkeeper went to take a goal kick in the dying seconds of the first half, but, as they say, "That's the way the wind blows." And the way the wind blew that day caught hold of the ball as he launched it up field with his goal kick. Far from ending up field, however, the strength of the wind took the ball, arcing it back from where it came so that it sailed unopposed into the net. It might have been less tragic had he realized immediately what had happened. But he didn't. Considering his immediate task had been completed with the taking of the goal kick, he turned round and slowly walked back toward his goal, with his back to play. It was only the loud roar — a cocktail of mirth, alarm, disbelief and despair — that drew his attention to the fact that all might not be well. So, he turned round to face the play in readiness to ward off any approaching challenge. He frantically looked for where the ball might be while his teammates collectively hollered, "Behind you!" He still assumed his goal was under attack so did not think to look in his own net for the ball. For a couple of moments, he dashed about like someone in a silent movie, his head jerking this way and that, in the manner of a puppet being worked by a drunk while he continued his frantic search for the ball. When he finally located it nestling in the back of his own net, his dignity was not enhanced when, in kicking the ball back up field for the match to restart, it once again blew back over him and went bouncing off far away behind the goal line.

Thus it was that we were three-nil down at half time, but now had the distinct advantage of playing with the wind. And after some five minutes, we scored. It was not a spectacular goal, nor one executed with flair and precision, but they all count: which is what our centre forward must have been feeling, as he tried to wipe the clump of mud off the back of his head, which is where the ball had struck him before entering the opponents' goal.

The score remained 3-1 for the next twenty minutes or so and we were not looking like scoring. Then their left winger disappeared, with the ball, into the crowd that was still encroaching onto the pitch. He was followed by the man in our team who was supposed to be marking him. I think it probably occurred to all the players and the referee at the same time that both players had gone missing for rather a long time. Shouts started to emerge from the crowd. Naturally curious, we wandered over. As we got close it became clear that a fight had broken out. Not to put too fine a point on it, our left wing and their man were trying to beat the crap out of each other. It was not long before the crowd started to take sides and some joined in. This gave me another memory to treasure: the sight of the referee running into the crowd and trying to get to and then separate two fighting players. I then noticed that the fight had now spread to some of the other players and it was all beginning to look a little ugly, a view shared by the referee. He fought his way out of the crowd, gave a sharp blast of his whistle and announced that the match was over. He stormed off the pitch without another word. And that was that. Match abandoned because of fighting between the teams. The fighting broke up soon enough and no one was seriously hurt. Even so, so much for 'Friendship First, Competition Second', I trudged wearily home to the Chinese Department wondering what Coach Wang—who had been invisible throughout the game—was going to say about the game at Monday's postmortem.

The answer was that he said a great deal at the postmortem but very little about the game itself. Instead, he turned to me and started talking and I soon became aware that he was talking for my benefit alone, although it took me a few moments to understand what he was talking about. The reason for this was that I had assumed he was talking about football, but after a minute or two floundering around in a swamp of misunderstanding, it dawned on me that Coach Wang was not talking about football at all. He was talking about food. And ration tickets. And then I gathered that I was being made a fully ledged member of the Fudan team and was therefore entitled to extra food ration tickets.

"To help build up your strength for the strenuous exertion of playing football."

So saying, he presented me with a book of tickets worth about ten *renminbi*.

"These can be used in the canteen. I suggest you buy eggs and extra meat with them," he added.

I felt a bit of a rogue accepting these ration tickets, as the foreign students were far better provided for than our Chinese fellow students. At Fudan, the local students got a monthly allowance of a measly seventeen *renminbi*, while we received several times more than that, as we received 120 per month. Nevertheless, I gratefully accepted the extra ration tickets.

After the post mortem, I returned elated to the Chinese Department and invited my two Chinese roommates to join me for supper at the canteen. I used my new ration tickets to order eggs all round. In fact, the three of us had eggs all round for the next few suppers. It was when I had only the ration ticket equivalent of one of the original ten *renminbi* left that I discovered that I had not fully comprehended what Coach Wang had been telling me. I had understood that members of the football team would receive these extra ration tickets monthly. Hence my largesse. However, my fellow teammate from the Chinese Department had seen me buying eggs like there was no tomorrow. He quietly informed me that the ration tickets were to last for the duration of an entire season and went on to explain the system in more detail. All Fudan students, he said, who were involved in active sport were given these extra ration tickets. They were to be used to buy eggs and meat on the night before the game and were to last the season. The ten *renminbi*, spread out over the length of the season meant an extra fifty cents to spend on the eve of a game. This extra fifty cents would buy you five eggs. I could now afford only ten more eggs to last the next four or five months.

I enjoyed my season's football playing for Fudan. It did not, however, lead to any real friendships with other members of the team, with the exception of K, who, in the end, only played in a few of the games. I did also become friends with three Romanian students who played for the Textile Institute. By the end of the season, I did at least know the names of my teammates, but there was no sense of belonging to the same team. The team members just went their separate ways after each game. Although, after one match towards the end of the season I went down to the local noodle shop with a couple of the other foreign students and came across four members of the team slurping away at noodles and happily quaffing beer. But it was rare to see local students at the noodle shop for reasons of expense. When your monthly allowance is a mere seventeen renminbi and buying enough ration tickets for three meals a day in the canteen costs fifteen renminbi per month, not many students had very much money left to spend on anything else. The sons and daughters of the rich and senior cadres were well off, of course, but in those days, the majority of university students comprised members of the three classes of peasants, workers and soldiers. There we no sons of senior cadres in the Fudan football team.

One person I did get to know quite well during the course of the season was the 'massage man'. He was the Chinese equivalent of the team's physiotherapist. I had to pay him several visits as I was being troubled by cramping in the thighs. So, I was sent to the 'massage man' for treatment. He looked harmless enough. Not a big man. Rather shy and wearing spectacles that were foreigners to fashion. But he could inflict pain.

"Please lie on this table," he invited me politely. I hobbled up to the table and sort of scrambled my way on to it.

"Where does it hurt?"

"Here...arrgghhh!" He found where it hurt right away.

Perhaps there was something addictive about the pain the 'massage man' was able to inflict, as I continued to visit him and mouth 'arrgghhh' during treatment.

I was confident in his ability to fix things, however. So, one morning when Lyn appeared walking as though she was trying to balance her head on her neck and complaining about neck pain, I immediately recommended him.

We entered his surgery. Lyn explained the problem. He walked around her a couple of times as though inspecting a prize lot at an auction.

"Sit down please." He beckoned to a cane chair that was standing alone in the middle of the room. Lyn sat.

"Take off your glasses." Lyn took them off, but a look of alarm was beginning to show on her face, as it was on mine.

The 'massage man' then stood behind Lyn, bent forward and put his left hand under her chin, cupping it, and his right hand on the back of her head. Then, suddenly, he jerked her head to the left. There was a loud disconcerting snap. I opened my eyes to see Lyn moving her head from side to side, and grinning with pleasure. One stiff neck fixed with a snap and a click.

The massage man's expertise was not always matched that of his colleagues in the medical profession. As everywhere, there were good and bad medics. We bumped into quite a few of the latter.

18

'WEAR MORE CLOTHES. DON'T CATCH COLD.'

There was — and probably still is — a belief in China, a belief shared by elderly peasant women down on the commune and doctors in main city hospitals that the more clothes you wear, the less likely you are to catch a cold. As any incipient sign of illness was initially classified as an upcoming cold, the visitor to China was constantly urged to 'Wear more clothes, don't catch cold.'

Most Chinese take this warning extremely seriously, if the amount of clothing worn by the average Chinese is anything to go by. During the cold winter months in Shanghai, it was not unusual for a person to wear no fewer than four pairs of trousers at the same time, along with several layers of clothing to protect the top half of the body, including vests and undershirts, shirts, sweaters, padded jackets and overcoats. On my first night with my new Chinese roommates, I watched with what started out as curiosity but slowly became incredulity tinged with awe, as one undressed for bed. First off was the padded jacket and the pair of padded trousers. Then two sweaters were removed until, eventually a cotton shirt appeared. This signaled it was time to remove the second pair of trousers, underneath of which were a pair of tracksuit bottoms. These were removed to reveal a rather fetching pair of woollen long johns. These remained on. Finally, off came the shirt revealing a thick vest. The vest and the long johns doubled as sleepwear. In a matter of minutes, I had seen a person whom I had taken to be of a sturdy build, diminish to one of scrawny straw-like thinness.

Coincidentally, a recent newspaper article related that Fidel Castro had launched a revolutionary campaign to get Cubans to wear fewer clothes and thus ease the strain on the Cuban textile industry. I figured the clothes worn by just one of my Chinese roommates would probably afford enough material to cloth a dozen Cubans. One man's revolution is another's chilblains and chattering teeth. The Cuban weather lends itself to skimpy outfits, the winter weather in 1976 Shanghai certainly did not. I also assumed that the amount of clothing that the average Chinese wore acted as something of a passion dampener. 'How many more layers?' one can imagine the ardent lover wondering in frustration.

Donning several layers of clothing may well keep the wearer warm during a miserable winter, but to what extent it decreases the wearer's likelihood of catching cold is less certain. The fact is that everyone, from the extremist seven-layer to the flighty two-layer chap, all caught them. What was certain, on the other hand, the amount of clothing being worn did little to lessen one's chances of contracting the hepatitis that was prevalent at the time. Proof of this was provided by a Canadian student, an early convert to the 'wear more clothes' school of health. He took himself off to the clinic complaining of general lethargy and a headache. He was immediately diagnosed as having caught a cold and was given the panacea to all ills, a glucose injection and the advice to 'wear more clothes.' Had the advice been taken, he would have been 'Michelin-manned' into a state of virtual immobility. Two days later, the man fainted in class and back to the clinic he went. This time the diagnosis was 'severe cold'.

A further injection of glucose was administered along with the admonition to 'rest more'.

It was only when the poor man could no longer summon the energy to leave his bed to perform his natural functions that it dawned on anyone that perhaps he had not caught a cold and that he might need more than more clothes. He was taken off to hospital, where hepatitis was diagnosed and where he stayed for several weeks before making a full recovery.

The next couple of weeks went by with everyone looking at each other, checking for traces of yellow in the whites of each other's eyes, one of the symptoms of the disease. People were unsure whether they felt lethargic or depressed because they were lethargic and depressed or because they had got hepatitis. Each pee was prefaced by fearful anticipation – would its color be brown, another symptom of the disease? A couple of other students did end up in hospital with suspected hepatitis, but it turned out that they had merely caught colds. One such, a Spanish chap, who was confined to his hospital bed for several days, kept insisting he felt perfectly fine. The day I went to visit him, he was sitting up in bed and playing his guitar – he had somehow managed to procure a single room – and dreaming of tortillas, not something that sufferers of hepatitis typically do. He was eventually discharged but his joy at being let out was short-lived. While walking along a street in town he suddenly doubled up in excruciating pain. A kidney stone had struck, so back to hospital he had to go.

Hepatitis scares came and went and we were periodically subjected to blood tests. It transpired that one of the reasons an unusually high number of foreign students from the West were diagnosed with the disease was apparently because Chinese give different blood count readings from Westerners. I was told that a white blood count that might signal hepatitis if detected in a Chinese patient represented a normal reading in Western patients. I am still not sure whether this is true or not, but it struck me as odd at the time. But what was really odd was the prophylactic measures that were adopted. As noted earlier, we were each given literally thousands of tiny pills, of which we were to take one hundred a day, thirty-three at both breakfast and lunch and thirty-four at supper. This extended meal times as we meticulously counted out these tiny pills. I still enjoy the memory of the sight of us, heads bowed over circular cardboard pillboxes, as we counted out our pills. They seemed to work, or at least did not do us any harm.

Healthy or not, there was no escape from the doctors, as we all had to have medicals. As, at the time, each administrative unit or place of work each required its own records, this meant we had to have a medical as soon as we arrived in at the Language Institute in Beijing and then another one when we arrived at Fudan. Having had to have a medical before leaving the UK for China, I thus had three medicals in three months, all of which meant three of everything including chest X-rays. In China we were also required to give stool and urine samples. My attempt to garner a stool sample for my Fudan medical did not go terribly well.

The doctor had given me a small cylindrical cardboard container with a twist off lid. Had it been made of tooled leather, I would have put my cufflinks in it. The doctor instructed me to return the cardboard cylinder the following day, with a stool sample within. Consequently, when I felt the urge arise, I dutifully traipsed off to the gents in the Chinese Department. These were of curious and unusual design. In addition to the urinals, there was a set of six cubicles and you had to climb up two concrete steps to reach them. Each cubicle had a wooden door but the wall to the cubicles did not reach the floor, but left a space of a couple of feet below the bottom of the wall and the level of the cubicles. This allowed one to see which of the cubicles were occupied. Once you had selected a free cubicle, you stepped up into it, closed the door and then had to straddle the trough that ran through all six cubicles and away into a main drain. There was a communal flush that operated periodically and washed away the collected waste in each of the cubicles. The flush announced itself with an ominous gurgling grumble before, suddenly, unleashing a flood.

This system of flushing naturally made the cubicle nearest the flush the most sought after, and the one furthest from it, the least. In cubicle one, if you timed it right, you only had your own waste to contend with. In cubicle six, if you were unlucky and a gurgling grumble announced an imminent flush while you were in mid-squat, you were treated to the sight of mountains of waste sluicing past beneath you.

On this day, I was unlucky as there were squatting feet visible in all but cubicle number five. I thus clambered aboard cubicle five, congratulating myself that I had thought to bring a long-handled spoon with me with which to scoop up a stool sample to scrape into my cardboard container. All went well and just as I was bending forward precariously with the long-handled spoon in one hand and the container in the other, I heard the incipient gurgling that signaled an oncoming communal flush.

Looking back on it, it was probably unwise to have tried to beat the flush. As it was, no sooner had I placed my spoon in position to collect my sample than all manner of waste and effluent raced past it. I had no desire to repeat an attempt at stool collecting, so I stoically drew up my spoon and scraped its contents into my little cardboard cylinder. I then trotted off to deliver it to the clinic. I am not sure whether my sample baffled the boffins, or whether my mongrel sample miraculously passed all the tests, but, very thankfully, I heard no more about it. Fortunately, both

Lyn and I remained healthy throughout our stay, and we both also lasted our time there without needing to go to the dentist.

19

A VISIT TO THE DENTIST

It was a great relief to me that I required no dental treatment while in China. Any planned visit to any dentist brings with it the anticipation of acute lancing pain as a drill bit hits a nerve. I think my lifelong fear probably stemmed from my compulsory visits to the dentist while at school. Our dentist went by the name of Miss Bonnet and was thought to be a marvelous dentist with the lightest of touches. Well, she may have been for others but, for some reason, I always experienced great discomfort whenever I sat in her dental chair. The result of this was, of course, that, in later life, I took to putting off going to the dentist until there was an obvious need to do so. Many is the time a dentist has let out a low whistle on seeing what damage has been visited upon my teeth, while prodding around and between them with an infernal tool that resembles a miniature pickax.

"Is this sensitive at all?"

"Aargghhh!" is the sort of conversation that tends to transpire while I was in the chair.

So, basically I used to shy away from dentists in general, but was always happy to accompany a friend who felt they needed some back-up support. So, when a Canadian student, D, at the Language Institute announced that he desperately needed to see a dentist and, as he had only been in China a couple of months, would need an interpreter, I volunteered for the position. I know one should not stereotype, but this Canadian was a very large specimen of lumbering lumberjack. He even wore one of those checked shirts that lumberjacks apparently favor.

The dental school was not far from the Institute so we cycled there. I soon realized that D was a man after my own lack of heart when it came to dentists, as the closer we came to the Dental School the more agitated he became. By the time we walked through the door, the man was a nervous wreck. I gathered from our conversation as we cycled to his appointment that his main fear centered around having a tooth extracted. This was interesting, as I did not mind that anything as much as the sound of a whining drill as one lay there helpless with palpitating heart, waiting for the excruciating shooting pain that was inevitably about to sear through you as the drill hit a nerve. He then told me this visit to the dentist had been deemed essential as he had begun to discharge bits of tissue from the gums beneath his lower front teeth. This sounded pretty ghastly to me, but D took some comfort from the thought that, at least, he was unlikely to have a tooth extracted. In the event, it turned out he was right, but I suspect that if he had known what was actually going to happen, he would have settled for having a tooth out every time.

We parked our bicycles and made our way into the Dental School, with D now literally shivering with fear. After some searching up and down corridors, we eventually located the dentist in question. It was a woman. D, being one of those very large men who become soppy and soft in the presence of females, took comfort from this fact. I thought that this was not the time to point out that the greatest pain I had experienced in a dental chair had been inflicted by a Miss Bonnet.

Before being asked to sit in the dental chair, the dentist started to address him. He looked plaintively and expectantly at me while she declaimed. The language of Chinese dentistry was not a facet of the language that I had studied in any depth. However, I was pretty confident that she was explaining that, first of all, she needed to 'investigate deeply' what the problem was. No mention of any teeth being extracted.

"She just wants to have a look first and then she'll explain what needs doing," I translated.

This seemed all right with D so he dragged himself to the chair, opened up and let her examine his mouth. She did this for a couple of minutes, and given there were no groans or cries of anguish, apparently painlessly—although D's knuckles showed white on the arms of the chair he was clutching. She then stood back, took me to one side, and whispered as though she was imparting confidential information the action she was going to take. I thought I had got the gist of this so told D.

"She's going to remove that stuff that's coming out of your gums and then put in some form of antiseptic to prevent infection."

"How?"

"How what?"

"How's she going to remove the stuff from my gums?"

I could see his point. The general drift might have been enough for the casual observer, but the patient needed more detail about the forthcoming operation.

"Don't worry," 'I said, "She said it would be quite simple and would not take long." I thought I had heard the word knife while she was speaking but thought it best not to mention this to D at this stage.

"Ah" said D, which was the last sound he was to make for the next 24 hours.

The dentist then instructed me to leave and wait in the waiting room. D protested, saying he needed me there to tell the dentist when he was in pain. I translated this and the dentist laughed as if to tell him not to be such a silly boy and then firmly ushered me out of the room.

I had only been in the waiting room for a couple of minutes when the dentist walked through, nodded at me, and a few seconds later walked back though the waiting room, nodding to me again. I had nodded back when she went through the first time but was reduced to gaping as she went back though the waiting room. She was holding out in front of her a tray upon which were arranged a whole series of cutting implements of various shapes and sizes. "Uh oh," I thought.

She had been as good as her word when she had said that it wouldn't take long. D was back in the waiting room within half an hour. The dentist told me to make sure D returned next week "to have the stitches removed".

D was silent, traumatized. His pre-treatment "Ah" was the last speech sound he made until the following day. Zombie-like he walked back to the Institute. I walked beside him pushing both bikes. He later told me he thought he had gone into shock when he saw the scalpels arrive on the tray. I can well believe it. They had been a nasty shock even for me when I saw them on their way through the waiting room. Happily, he had felt no pain and, importantly, it turned out that the dentist had done a first-class job. A problem that had been bothering him for three years gave no further problems.

When he went to have his stitches removed, he did not ask me to accompany him as his interpreter.

20

'DON'T STAND AROUND STARING AT FOREIGNERS'

I mentioned earlier the student from the North African country to whom fate had been unkind and who found himself enrolled at the Beijing Language Institute. Fate had been especially unkind as he was on holiday in Beijing where his father was his country's ambassador. At the time, the Chinese authorities were offering a number of scholarships for third-world students and five had been offered to this particular country. Embarrassingly, only three applications were received. The ambassador, in order to make up the numbers, volunteered his holidaying son. Thus it transpired that an extremely privileged and wealthy son of a North African ambassador had his holiday in Beijing rudely interrupted. He was enrolled in the Language Institute and, once he had passed his language exams, would be enrolled in the Textile Institute. Sadly 'A' did not prove to be a good student of the Chinese language, so he spent two full years at the Language Institute before graduating to study textiles. He proved a poor student at that too, so was to fail his first-year exams there two years running. He had thus spent four years in China with the prospect of at least a further three. Life was made even harder for him for, on a specially sanctioned R&R trip to Hong Kong, he managed to contract a nasty case of venereal disease. This was discovered by the Chinese, so he was forbidden to leave China again until he had completed his studies. This travel ban was lifted, as he was allowed to visit his father who had since been posted to another country. However, his father forced him to return. When I left China, 'A' was wrestling for the third time with his first-year exams at the Textile Institute. This time he passed them. Fate had indeed been unkind. A few weeks' holiday in Beijing had turned into what must have seemed to him like a five-year prison sentence, with at least two more years to serve.

Although 'A' was by no means typical of the third-world students, he shared one thing in common with the majority, and that was they wanted to get out of China. As noted earlier, very few were in China of their own accord. Many were there because they had failed to get scholarships to study elsewhere and several had been, like 'A', volunteered for political and diplomatic reasons. Others were there because they had been given the wrong information about the nature of their courses. For example, they had been told that they would be able to study their subject in either French or English. It was only after their arrival that they were disabused of this and informed they would have to study their subjects in Chinese—and that this meant an additional year at least at the Language Institute studying Chinese. It was also rare for them to be able to get home at any time during their time in China. It is not surprising that so many were so keen to get out.

In addition to the usual frustrations of living in China, there were other causes for concern as exemplified by the disturbing case of the medical student from an African country and his illicit night of love. This was indeed a bizarre and deeply unsettling story. He was one day invited by one of his Chinese roommates to spend the day—a Sunday—at his home. This in itself was very unusual, if not unheard of. Our man was in line for something unusual all right. He spent some twenty-four hours at his roommate's home, but not with him, but alone in a room with a girl provided by his roommate. When he returned to the Medical Institute where his friends were anxiously wondering whether some accident had befallen him, they immediately discerned by the grin of his face that what had happened to him had been enjoyable.

There the matter rested. Until, some five months later, he received a communication from the bureaucrats of the Medical Institute which contained a statement that outlined his activities during those twenty-four hours he had spent at his roommate's home. The bureaucrats demanded that he sign it, otherwise, he would be sent home. This, of course, was a feeble threat, as being sent home could be seen as a prize. But, bravely, he refused to sign it. A sort of Mexican stand-off then ensued with his being told to sign the statement and refusing to do so. After several days of this, the authorities caved in and he was allowed to stay without having to sign the statement. But what was deeply upsetting about the case was that, apparently, the statement documented precisely, in intimate detail, what had occurred at his roommate's house.

This feeling of being under constant surveillance was felt by us all. My own two roommates, with whom, fortunately, I got along well, openly admitted that they had to attend a weekly meeting with the bureaucracy at which all Chinese students who had foreign roommates were expected to report back what had been said. So this feeling of being constantly monitored was not based on paranoia.

On top of this unsettling feeling of being observed and reported on, more trivial nuisances constantly occurred. For example, an ad hoc party that developed in one of the bedrooms was interrupted at nine in the evening by the authorities who argued that, as all Chinese students were to be in bed by nine, then the party needed to stop then and there. That is was utter nonsense to claim that the Chinese students all went to bed at nine only served to make what was, in essence, a minor incident, inflammatory. Harsh words and insults were exchanged.

These unpleasant shouting matches between foreign students and the university bureaucrats became almost daily occurrences. This was hardly surprising, as we were allowed to do very little without their permission; and they seldom gave permission, often without providing any reason or by proffering some absurd nonsensical one. We therefore organized events without seeking permission. Naturally, they found out about these. Further rows ensued. These were not without their moments of humor, however. On one occasion we organized a dance and invited the Department caretaker to attend, which, to our surprise and delight he did. The dance was soon 'raided' by members of the bureaucracy. The caretaker then provided a fantastic example of how to survive politically in an authoritarian state. One second he was joking and sharing a beer with us. The next, apparently off the cuff, he stood up and produced an extraordinary diatribe against the West and its evil influences. He signaled out dancing as being an exemplar of Western corruption, actually calling dance "an evil and corrupting capitalist bourgeois trait," All this for the ears of the bureaucrats. He was successful, as he retained his caretaker's job.

This incident also caused another darkly humorous episode. I had written an article about the dance for the *Far Eastern Economic Review*, under the title "A new tune but no dancing". Shortly after its publication, my two roommates approached me looking sheepish and shamefaced. Could I help them translate the article I had written into Chinese? They had been asked to do this by the authorities and their English was far too poor to be able to do this unaided. So I found myself in the farcical position of helping my 'monitors' escape censure themselves by assisting them in their spying duties.

The foreign students all had similar frustrations to face. The African students also had to contend with racial prejudice. In fact, the Chinese had a hierarchy of racial prejudice. At the top were the Han Chinese themselves; white westerners came next followed by South Asians, then 'other' Asians and people from the Middle East. Blacks, people of color as we now say, came at the bottom of the Chinese ladder of racial prejudice. This prejudice, combined with the Chinese tendency at the time to stare at anything that looked unusual, combined to make the lives of many of the African students a misery. Every time a group of African students left their campus to go into town, they would be immediately surrounded by a crown of gawping Chinese. The crowds were not aggressively hostile, but to be stared at by a jostling, shoving crowd of Chinese must have been a deeply upsetting experience. The threat of these gawping crowds restricted many African students to their campuses. A call that had been made earlier by Zhou Enlai that Chinese "should not surround and stare at foreigners" went unheeded.

I mentioned earlier that, for the African students, China was like a prison sentence, with so many freedoms restricted. In stark contrast, for many of the Middle Eastern students, China represented some form of liberal paradise. Alcohol was freely available and, not only could one see girls, one could actually talk to them. Perhaps not surprisingly, some Middle Eastern students went overboard. On one occasion, Lyn and I were attending a private party where alcohol was served and a student from North Yemen who had imbibed too freely, made a lunge for Lyn and tried to embrace and kiss her. He was the only person I have ever actually punched in anger. The punch floored him and he desisted.

With dances and other types of entertainment officially outlawed, the only celebration and excuse for a party were the respective national days. These the Chinese themselves felt obliged to celebrate 'for the friendship of our two nations'. Such celebrations would begin with the Chinese making hypocritical speeches extolling the great friendship between the two nations, hypocritical because the students from whatever nation whose national day was being celebrated were actually not allowed to make friends with Chinese.

Occasionally, a National Day celebration proved worth attending. One such was Sudan's National Day. On its National Day 1977, Sudan was celebrating the eighth anniversary of Gaafar Nimeiry's presidency. The first thing that captured the eye on entering the Hall where the National Day was being celebrated was the sight of three official portraits. In addition to the customary two of Mao and Hua, there was also one of Nimeiry himself. His portrait made a startling contrast to those of Mao and Hua. They were wearing their sombre gray Mao suits. Nimeiry, on the other hand, was in full the military regalia of his Field Marshall's rank, with a chest and torso festooned with medals and decorations. One earnest Sudanese told me, pointing at the most colorful of Nimeiry's chest accessories, that this was the medal 'for evacuation'. I am still not quite sure what the medal was for.

Part of the hall had been set aside for a small exhibition of photos from Sudan. These displayed Sudanese, smiling happily, working in the fields. There were photographs of major earthworks and irrigation schemes, of factories, of 'progress'. All very Chinese, in fact. Even Lyn's and my great Sudanese friend, Big Foot, apparently seriously, explained that "these photographs portray people learning to love labor."

Perhaps I should explain how our friend got his name. First, he had prodigiously large feet; so large, in fact, that he was unable to find shoes or sandals in China that would come close to fitting. When he learned that Lyn and I were going to Hong Kong, he asked whether we would buy him some shoes and send them to him. Of course, we said, but how would we know what size and shape of shoe to buy. As if anticipating this problem, he promptly withdrew a large piece of paper from his pocket on which he had traced an outline of his right foot.

'If you can find sandals to fit this foot, please buy three pairs.'

When we later got to Hong Kong, Lyn and spent some splendid moments with our large piece of paper sourcing sandals in shoe shops. A typical exchange would go

"What you want?"

"We are looking for a pair of sandals."

"For you or her?"

"For this," so saying we would unfurl the paper bearing Big Foot's tracing

"Wha!" (a common Cantonese exclamation expressing awe and wonder) "So big. No have."

Eventually we had three pairs of sandals made for him.

Anyway, back to Sudan Day.

Having been escorted round the photographs depicting Sudan's revolution, we took our seats at long wooden tables upon which had been placed the typical National Day celebratory fare. This included biscuits, peanuts, boiled sweets, pitchers of orange cordial and bowls full of expensive filter-tipped cigarettes. Some teetotal toasting then followed. Then came the speeches. The first, given in Arabic by a Sudanese student and translated into Mandarin by a second student was overtly political. The speaker drew his largest round of applause when he attacked Zionism and praised, most fulsomely, the Palestinian cause. There were many Arab students in the room and a few Palestinians. Any Zionists present weren't saying.

The Chinese response was given by a member of the relevant university's bureaucracy. He spent most of his time laying into the Gang of Four. His rambling did eventually come close to being relevant to the fact it was Sudan's National Day when he concluded by stressing the importance of China's deep friendship with the third world and how they must unite against the imperialism of the first and second world nations. It was then that I realized Lyn and I were the only second-worlders present. I whitely and obviously so. I shifted a little uncomfortably in my seat with the feeling that all Arab and Chinese eyes were now staring aggressively in my direction.

The speeches over, it was time for the entertainment. And we were treated to a bewildering display. First up was a dance performed by the Sudanese students, with Big Foot vainly trying to appear light of foot and Lyn and I vainly trying not to giggle as our friend clumped around the wooden stage. Then, up shot a Palestinian who launched into an impromptu speech expressing undying solidarity with Sudan when the poor chap froze, speechless. All his Chinese had suddenly and momentarily been forgotten or become unobtainable. He finished his speech in Arabic. Third, the Albanian students stood up and sang an Albanian folk song. This was greeted with polite but baffled applause. Not to be outdone, up-stepped the Sri Lankans with a folk song and then it was the turn of the Yemenis. I was now naturally getting extremely nervous unless all eyes turned to me and I was asked to perform a 'typical folk song from your country'. Thankfully, as soon as the Yemenis had finished their song, a Zairois took the stage and delivered a monologue. The man was a comic genius as no one apart from his compatriots could understand a word of what he was saying — he must have been using some local pidgin or creole, but he somehow had us hooting with laughter. He was followed by the Palestinians again, this time with a song. Then the Chinese chipped in. Then a Syrian ditty from the Syrian contingent. Then up stood the three Nepalese and sang us a song of Nepal. By now, I was naturally becoming panic-stricken at the thought that I might have to give a rendition of *On Ilkley Moor Ba T'at*, a stirring Yorkshire folk song sung in local dialect, the title of which means 'On Ilkley Moor without a hat'. Mercifully, at this stage the student from Togo, unbidden, stood up and sang a song. Finally, there was a sort of Arab choral ensemble. Or, it should have been finally but, displaying an imperfect sense of timing, the Pakistani students then sang. After which the Sudan National Day celebrations were declared closed and the attendees mercifully spared a rendition of *On Ilkley Moor Ba T'at*.

Despite the presence of several members of the Chinese bureaucracy on these occasions, relationships between them and the foreign students remained tense and unpleasant. In a way this had a positive outcome because it united the foreign students against 'them', the Chinese bureaucracy. I am sure Lyn and I would have been able to make all the friends we did with our fellow students had times been more relaxed and we had been allowed to form friendships with the Chinese themselves. Having said that, being now able to look back on more than fifty years' experience working in universities and with international students, it remains true that international students are more likely to make friends with each other than with local students, perhaps because they share the experience of traveling overseas and studying in what is to them a foreign language and in what is to them an 'alien' culture. Local students can seem rather dull in comparison.

Some of our own entertainments were approved by the

bureaucrats. One such was the 'Davis' cup tennis tournament played over several months between Britain (Lyn and me) against Romania (any pairing of the three Romanian students). The Romanians presented a fascinating trio of contrasts. One spoke English, one French, the other German—all could, of course, speak their own language and Chinese. Conversations with them as a group could become linguistically confusing, especially after the consumption of the beer and wine much favored by both teams. Romania eventually emerged victorious, but only narrowly.

The routine of life was seldom disturbed by events of external significance. But for the four British students at Fudan, an event of external significance certainly interrupted the humdrum routine of campus life. This was the visit to the university by the then leader of the British Conservative Party, which was then in opposition, Margaret Thatcher.

21

THE IRON LADY AT FUDAN

The Fudan bureaucracy ran pretty true to form by not giving the four British students any information at all regarding Mrs Thatcher's visit. Indeed, had we not been told by the British Embassy that she intended to visit Fudan, she might have come and gone without any of us realizing it. As it was, we knew both that she was coming to Fudan and the day on which she was scheduled to visit. Even then, and even knowing that we knew, the university still refused to acknowledge that Mrs Thatcher was due to visit. We were able to get the university to confess that she was coming by suggesting we made posters to hang out of our windows saying the equivalent of 'Down with Mrs Thatcher!' This mischievous idea was greeted seriously and with abject horror by the authorities, thereby admitting she was indeed coming to visit.

The Great Day dawned and my first surprise was to see our Chinese roommates scrubbing away and dusting down our bedrooms. There was similar activity throughout the Department. Even the lavatories were getting a thorough once over. The thought of the Leader of the Opposition having to use these was pleasurably amusing.

That this Great Cleansing was taking place in our Department suggested, even to the dimmest among us, that Mrs T was going to visit the Department. Would she be taking tea with us as well? No, as it happened, and neither did she visit the Department. The Great Cleansing was in vain.

The university authorities continued to refuse to divulge when exactly she was due to arrive. They clearly did not want us anywhere near her, presumably in case she heard some unpalatable truths about life in China from us. We therefore spend the morning hanging around the main gate waiting for the official entourage to arrive. Arrive it duly did, and then the fun began.

She, together with her daughter Carol, who was accompanying her on the trip, were first whisked off for the official speeches of welcome, when she was no doubt told how much better life in China and Fudan was since the liberation, since the Great Proletarian Cultural Revolution, since the fall of the Gang of Four etc, etc, etc. We took the opportunity to renew friendships and acquaintances with British Embassy staff and Beijing-based journalists who were also part of the entourage. One particular journalist friend who, with his wife, on learning that we were not allowed to live together had been thoughtful and kind enough to ask Lyn and I to stay overnight with them on occasion while we were still in Beijing, had a particular story to tell about a contretemps with Mrs Thatcher. He had briefed her before her visit with Chairman Hua and gave her some details about Hua's son and what he was studying and so forth. When it came to the meeting, Mrs Thatcher asked after Hua's son, but got some of the details about him wrong, and Hua corrected her. She apparently then turned to the journalist in question – who was seated, along with other journalists, in the same room and said "Never give me false information again!"

When the journalist later sought an apology, explaining

that she had mistaken what he had told her, she sternly and unequivocally replied,

"I have a mind like a filing cabinet. I never make mistakes."

The welcome speeches over, she was led off to visit the library. The four British students followed along in her wake, ignoring all gestures and signs from the Chinese that we should disappear.

The reason why our presence was not welcome became immediately apparent as we entered the library. This was a very different library from the one we had grown to loathe. The first thing to catch the eye as we wandered into the main reading room was the number of foreign up-to-date newspapers and magazines that were lying around. In the several months we had been at Fudan, we had not seen a single foreign newspaper in the library. Now suddenly the *Economist, the Far Eastern Economic Review, The Times*, the *Guardian Weekly* and others were all openly displayed. For all the world, it looked as though popping into the library after lunch to catch up with foreign news was a regular routine.

On seeing this display, Mrs Thatcher turned to us and asked in a loud voice that could be heard by the University Rector and the rest of the party.

"Are these papers here every day?"

"No", we chorused, "Not every day. Not any day."

Whereupon Mrs Thatcher turned a steely gaze at the Rector, a steely and deeply unsettling gaze that, in time, would become universally familiar, especially to members of her own Cabinets.

We then moved on to the library catalogue. Now, it has to be said the Fudan library catalogue was impressive and the library was extremely well stocked, although the great majority of books were stowed away in the stacks, where the shelves could not be browsed by actual users of the library. The problems arose when readers actually wanted to borrow a book. They would check the catalogue, then go to the desk to ask for the book or books in question to be brought up from the stacks. For example, let's say a reader had seen that the library catalogue showed that it had a copy of *Inner Asian Frontiers* by Owen Lattimore. He would go off to the desk, fill in the loan form which he would then hand to the librarian who would disappear into the darkness of the stacks. After a passage of time, the librarian would eventually reappear and announce with a straight face,

"It's already been borrowed"

"Can I reserve it?"

"Yes," says the librarian.

But, mysteriously, the book was never recalled and was always 'out'. This farce was repeated whenever someone tried to borrow a book. A new Murphy's Law came into force. "Whatever book you want to borrow, that book is and always will be 'Out'. "

This then explains why we were so grateful when Mrs Thatcher said that she wanted to visit the stacks. The Chinese tried to dissuade her ("It's dark, it's dirty, it's a little dangerous," they squeaked), but she stood firm. Much to the consternation of the authorities in general and the Head Librarian in particular, we duly traipsed down into the stacks. Mrs Thatcher was clearly aware of why we wanted time there, so spent a good twenty minutes there giving us time to feverishly note down as many titles of as many books that we could in the time.

The following day, we went to the library and filled out our loan forms, now knowing that the books were there and knowing that the librarian knew we knew that they were there. We did wonder whether, despite all, he would return from the stacks and apologetically explain that they were all out. But he didn't. Instead he returned from the stack pushing a large trolley replete with the books we had requested. Thanks to Mrs Thatcher, therefore, we were finally able to borrow books from the library.

But the newspapers never returned.

Following her visit to the library, Mrs Thatcher was taken to see an English class in action. The standard of English among Fudan's English majors was not, generally speaking, very high, although there were a few who had attended a leading cadres' school whose English was extraordinarily good. For example, on one occasion when I was walking on my own across a campus a young man approached me. Before I could put on my "I'm Finnish, I'm afraid I don't speak English," act, he asked me in impeccable British English.

"Do you happen to know anything about the Elizabethan navy? You see, I'm doing research on it and was wondering whether you could help me?"

Sadly, I couldn't. It was only later when I thought I should have asked him which Elizabeth. I assume he had meant Elizabeth II.

In general, however, levels of English proficiency were low. One essay I was fortunate enough to come across while it was pinned to a noticeboard and which had a red carnation—the mark of excellence—stuck to it, read in part:

"An advanced class was held in an advanced girl's bedroom and two advanced girls were chosen."

Grammatically flawless.

The class that Mrs Thatcher saw had clearly been rehearsed. As was typical of all such classes visited by foreign dignitaries, not only the language but also the content of the class had been rehearsed. The content chosen for Mrs Thatcher's ears had been selected to leave her in no doubt as to where the English Department at Fudan stood on the subject of the Soviet Union. A sample of the dialogue:

Student A: "Why can't the Soviet people afford butter?"

Student B: "Because the Soviet Revisionists spend all their

money on tanks."

The question of what to talk about in English classes was felt by all teachers and students at the time. Students were being taught to say things such as, "Our great and glorious leader" and got their information about the English speaking world through situational dialogues with titles like 'At the dole queue', but little else.

It was fascinating to see how the Chinese tried to deal with a foreign 'personage' and equally fascinating to see how Mrs Thatcher dealt with the Chinese. She made it crystal clear that she did not believe the propaganda and guff that she was being showered with. She also made it crystal clear that she was angry at being treated as a gullible fool.

In contrast, certain members of the Western press who formed part of the entourage betrayed their lack of any understanding of China as the following examples illustrate. The first incident occurred as the British film crew were setting up their cameras on the university campus. It should be remembered that the Chinese at Fudan were not used to seeing foreigners. They had just about got used to the presence of foreign students on the campus. The arrival, therefore, on campus of a whole heap of foreigners, who included dignitaries, diplomats and journalists was an unprecedented event and one that had to be observed at close hand. In addition, if you walked around the campus with a non-Chinese made camera hanging round your neck, the Chinese would be desperately curious and want to look at it. So the presence of two foreign TV film crews with their sophisticated-looking television cameras was, for the Chinese, a truly mind-blowing spectacle. They immediately crowded round the cameras, started to stroke them in awe while peering closely into the lenses. This was obviously going to make the filming of the arrival of Mrs Thatcher tricky. So, the director of one of the film crews called out to his interpreter,

"I say, Mr Li, do you think you could ask these chaps to walk up and down naturally in front of that statue over there"? That statue over there being the statue of Mao.

Interpreter Li looked taken aback, as well he might. He must have wondered how long it would be before people to whom he had been assigned would start to get an inkling about China and stop asking him to do things that were both silly and clearly impossible.

The second example which betrayed certain journalists' lack of knowledge about China occurred with their attempt to find some local Chinese to interview. In this most were hampered by not speaking a word of Chinese. Imagine the sense of triumph, therefore, when one such journalist, a blustery fellow with a face lined with red veins that suggested an appreciation of the bottle, unearthed a Chinese student who not only spoke fluent English but also seemed remarkably open about expressing her negative feelings about China. He could hardly believe his luck and out came his notebook as he feverishly jotted away, trying to get as much out of his source before any of the other journalists picked up on what was happening. On finishing his surreptitious interview, he smugly pocketed his notebook. In his triumph, it had not occurred to him to wonder how it was that a Chinese student spoke such idiomatic English, was prepared to be critical of China and was wearing clothes that were clearly distinct from the clothes that were worn by Chinese students. I took some pleasure in informing George Gale, the journalist in question, that he had just interviewed Lyn.

Mrs Thatcher only spent a morning at Fudan, but she left her mark and the university authorities can have been in no doubt that she was deeply unimpressed by them and their posturing. Her parting remark to the four British students gives, perhaps, a slight insight into the character of this remarkable woman. Just before she climbed back into her official car, the then Leader of the Opposition walked over to us and said, sotto voce,

"When you get back, do drop in, Number Ten, talk about China."

22

'YOU SHOULD HEAR WHAT THEY DID TO ME!'

On May 26, there appeared a wall poster written by some
second-year students in the Chinese Department. The wall
poster recorded, in some detail, the ordeal undergone by one of
their fellow students, a girl called Zhang Jinhua. Zhang, while
still a first-year student, had taken it upon herself to write to
officials in her home village and to the authorities at Fudan
University itself. According to the wall poster, in both letters she
had 'complained about the Gang of Four'. And, as a result of
her two letters, 'investigation was carried out against her.' She
was promptly placed under room-arrest at Fudan for a month
and two people were given the task of 're-educating' her. One of
these two people was a fellow student in the Chinese Department
and whose name had appeared as one of the signatories of the
wall poster. The wall poster called upon those who had been
responsible for her arrest and interrogation to repent.

Although this incident was comparatively trivial, given the
appalling treatment that others had suffered over this period,
the essence of the case was intriguing. A student writes a couple
of letters to the authorities protesting against the policies of
the Gang of Four. As a result, she is placed under room-arrest,
interrogated and re-educated by two people, one of whom is a

classmate. None of her other classmates come to her defence. Most quietly accept what has happened. A few add accusations. Then, a year later, the girl in question is hailed as a heroine by those who had initially, at best, ignored her plight. The girl herself reported that she felt no ill will towards her fellow students. On the contrary, she felt that it was only natural that her friends had not stood up for her.

Most of us found this very difficult to understand: that she bore no ill will; that she did not think her fellow students' actions despicable now that they were clamoring about what a wonderful person she was, when it was politically safe, even expedient, for them to do so.

From about this time, every visit we made to a factory or place of designated interest, some person or other was wheeled out, often literally, to give us a recitation of how they had suffered under the Gang of Four and how deliriously grateful they were to Chairman Hua and his wise leadership.

As had been the case on our visit to Lu Xun's hometown, the person in question would usually be a frail, elderly woman, with white hair, almost colourless eyes and a face etched with pain and anguish. (White hair, colourless eyes, which the Chinese actually call blue, are de rigeur for long sufferers.) The white hair bespeaks grief, the colorless eyes are the eyes that have become blind from the weeping of so many tears. At the beginning of her recital, the 'victim' would almost, but never, quite, become too overcome by grief to continue. She would recover to catalogue list upon list of the heinous crimes committed by the Gang of Four and their henchmen.

If all this sounds a little cynical, it is because the same victim seemed to be telling the same stories wherever we went. And the stories and their narrators soon became, in my mind at least, lampoons and caricatures riddled with cliché. This apparent

Chinese need to make these recitations a form of performance art diminished the suffering felt by people who had really fallen foul of the Gang of Four. These ranged from students such as Zhang Jinhua and famous novelists, such as Ba Jin.

Ba Jin came to Fudan in June 1977 to give a talk to the foreign students of Chinese Literature. The story of how it was that he actually came to visit us shed light on the workings of the Chinese bureaucratic mind and CCP cadres.

While we were still in Beijing, I had been told by a member of the British Embassy that Ba Jin was, if not well, alive and living in Shanghai.

When we had first arrived at Fudan in early September, I had therefore asked whether it would be possible for us to meet the famous Ba Jin. The conversation went like this.

'We hear that Ba Jin, the wonderful novelist, is living in Shanghai. For the students of Chinese literature, it would be a wonderful honor for us to be able to meet him. We have studied his works and know he is a true giant of literature."

"Who told you about Ba Jin?"

"A member of my Embassy."

"You have been told lies. You cannot meet Ba Jin."

Why not?'

"Because he is dead."

There was little chance of any compromise here. A person is either dead or alive; we could hardly have left the meeting agreeing that, while alive, he was dead. As it turned out, that compromise would have been possible, as this is what the bureaucracy told us when, in February, we made our second request to meet him. The fact that we were permitted to approach the bureaucracy with this second request was, in itself, telling. For the second request, no mention was made of the 'fact' that he was dead. This time, the conversation, started in the same way and went like this,

"We hear that Ba Jin, the wonderful novelist, is living in Shanghai. For the students of Chinese literature, it would be a wonderful honor for us to be able to meet him. We have studied his works and know he is a true giant of literature."

"There is perhaps a serious problem."

"What problem?"

"Ba Jin is suffering from a long-term illness and is not well enough to meet people."

Encouraged by this Lazarus-like resurrection, we asked for a third time in May.

"We hear that Ba Jin, the wonderful novelist, is living in Shanghai. For the students of Chinese literature, it would be a wonderful honor for us to be able to meet him. We have studied his works and know he is a true giant of literature."

There followed a pause during which a couple of members of the bureaucracy whispered among themselves. Then one looked up and said,

"We have decided that it would be an excellent idea for you to meet one of China's most celebrated authors, Ba Jin. Would you foreign students like to meet him?"

"Yes, indeed."

"Very good!" they crowed. "We shall arrange this."

The saga of the Ba Jin requests had given us an exemplary lesson in the distinction between actual death and political death. From being politically dead and persona non grata in November 1976, by May 1976, Ba Jin had become politically rehabilitated.

Thus it was that Ba Jin came to talk to us in June. The first feeling that most of us had during our discussion with him was relief that the discussion was not going to be a monologue that itemised a list of evils perpetrated by the Gang of Four. It was also a relief that he was happy to talk about himself and his role in Chinese literature. The Gang of Four did not escape unscathed, however. One of the four, Zhang Chunqiao, came in for special mention. He was accused of wishing the Chinese people to be 'people of no education', 'illiterates who understood nothing'. He also noted that it had been the Gang of Four who had spread rumors of his death. That might have disturbed the members of the university bureaucracy who were present, but they, survivors all, nodded sagely, clucked sympathetically and agreed it was dreadful how people could descend to such levels of duplicity.

Ba Jin had always been a student of anarchism and it has always been assumed that his pen name derived from the first syllable of Bakunin's and the final syllable of Kropotkin's names. Ba Jin contradicted this, saying that while the Jin was indeed derived from the final syllable of Kropotkin's name, the Ba had been taken from the name of a Chinese friend who had committed suicide while studying in Paris in the 1920s, when Ba Jin himself was a student there. As the Chinese press had just published an article reassessing Bakunin's role in the Russian revolution and dubbed him an 'irresponsible nihilist' I did wonder whether Ba Jin was distancing himself from the work of Bakunin.

Ba Jin had published his last novel in 1962. We were all obviously keen to know whether he intended writing any new fiction. He replied that he was currently working on a fourth volume of his famous trilogy of novels, *Family, Spring and Autumn*. The fourth volume was to be called *The Masses* and would deal with life before the liberation. This seemed a politically contrived title to keep the authorities happy. In any event, the fourth volume of the trilogy has never appeared.

His view of literature was that it should educate the masses and confine itself to their needs. This was a particularly hard task for an intellectual such as himself, as he was too far removed from the everyday life of the masses. Predictably, therefore, he suggested the Chinese literature of the 1950s and 1960s had reached a higher level of attainment than the literature of his own era, the pre-liberation 1930s. But then, in direct contradiction to what he had just said, he singled out his contemporaries, Mao Dun, Cao Yu and Lu Xun as being the most important Chinese authors of the 20th Century. Anyone but Ba Jin would have probably added his name to that list.

While I had felt relief at the beginning of the discussion that Ba Jin had avoided listing a litany of Gang of Four crimes and mouthing inane clichés, by the time the discussion was over I was left with a feeling of sadness. While he had not mouthed inane clichés he had not done much more. I found it impossible to rid myself of the suspicion that he had been rehabilitated and allowed 'out' to provide evidence of the more liberal attitudes of the Hua regime and on the condition that he support the regime in his public utterances and writing. Yet, despite this, there was a twinkle in the great man's eye and he smiled and laughed readily. This in itself was the sign of a person of humanity with a talent for forgiveness. This was a man who had been forced to kneel on shards of broken glass while confessing to confected crimes during the Cultural Revolution. He went on to live a long life. Born in 1904, he was seventy-three when he visited Fudan. While he published no more fiction, he did publish five volumes of *Random Thoughts* between 1978 and 1986. He was also, for a while, chairman of the Chinese Writers' Association', proof that he had been fully rehabilitated. He suffered ill health in the last years of his life, but lived until he was 100.

That Ba Jin had been given permission to talk to foreign students at Fudan was certainly a sign of a more liberal regime. As people began to feel more comfortable that the Hua regime had indeed managed to 'smash' the Gang of Four, so did people feel more comfortable about denouncing people at whose hands they had suffered under them. It was get-even time, or, as the Chinese say, time to settle accounts.

June 1977 was a month of trials and mass criticism sessions. The accused, often identified in wall posters that were pasted up in various parts of the city, including Fudan's own 'Wall poster Alley', were paraded around the city and brought before 'the masses' in factories and other institutions where their crimes were read out. Further accusations could be leveled at the accused by members of the crowd.

On Saturday June 25, all the Chinese students left the Department at 6:00 a.m. in the morning and went off to a local sports stadium to attend one of these mass criticism sessions. The foreign students had also tried to attend but, not surprisingly, were forbidden to do so. I am indebted to a student from the Chinese Department for the following summary of what took place.

There were three accused at this particular session, namely Xu Jingxian, Wang Xiuzhen and Zhu Yongjia. All were well known figures in Shanghai politics. They were led into the stadium and were forcibly pushed down on three chairs. A 'chairman' then invited members of the audience to raise any allegations they might have against any or all of the three accused. About fifty people took this opportunity. The first person to make an allegation was a student from Fudan's Foreign Languages Department, and the great majority of the later accusations followed similar lines. The accusations alleged that people who had opposed Zhang Chunqiao in the 1960s had been targeted by Zhang and his henchmen. Zhang had established an elaborate organization to weed out those who had criticized him. The three on trial were all key members of this organization. They were accused of locking people up, some for several years, with several of those imprisoned committing suicide. Others had been murdered by their jailers. Any lucky enough to be released were given a record that basically made it impossible for them to get any work. This criticism session lasted several hours as the three accused listened to this stream of allegations.

It was impossible to discover what sentences each of the accused received, but three outcomes from these mass criticism sessions were common: suicide; a death sentence and for crimes considered less severe, re-education.

There was no such uncertainty around the punishment for common criminals as opposed to politicals. My two roommates also attended what was known as an 'area trial', so-called as criminals were tried in the region where they had committed the crime. This trial was also held in the local sports stadium. This was jam-packed with spectators by the time the trucks containing the accused arrived. There were eleven accused who were escorted to the center of the arena by members of the militia and Public Security Bureau, these being armed. The crimes of the accused were then read out to the assembled masses. Sentences passed with the audience baying approval or disapproval at the sentences being passed, but without influencing the sentences set down. One of the eleven was sentenced to death. Death sentences had to be referred to Beijing.

The foreign students were never allowed into the sports stadium to witness a trial, either political or criminal. But on the very afternoon of the political trial, we were taken there to see a soccer match between the PLA and Athens. Athens won 2-0.

23

A SPECIAL EXAM

A local newspaper report, which I translate in full below, recounted the following.

> One day towards the end of April 1977, a secondary school student from Beijing's 112 Secondary School, was sweeping out a classroom when a sudden gust of wind blew up. The doors and windows of the classroom started banging and it looked as though the glass in the windows was in danger of smashing. The student, a girl called Yuan Fang, rushed over to the windows to secure them. She arrived too late, however, and the shattering glass badly cut her right hand. The school rushed her off to hospital where a doctor put eight stitches in the cut, told her to take time off school and rest her hand.
>
> All this was particularly upsetting for Yuan Fang, for the school exams were due to start the following day. Yuan Fang wanted to be a true Party member and saw this crisis as an opportunity to the Party and people of China to examine her and to see how conscientious a student she was. Some of her friends

advised her to forget the exams and not bother with
them this time round. To this, Yuan Fang replied, "I
simply cannot hand in nothing." Her friends then
pointed out that it could not be considered 'handing in
nothing' as she had severely damaged her right hand.
"Do a make-up exam later." they urged her. But Yuan
Fang wouldn't hear of it.

"This is the first set of exams since the smashing of
the Gang of Four by the Party under Chairman Hua's
leadership. How then can I refuse to sit the exams and
thus deny the Party and the People the chance to see
how I've been doing?"

Yuan Fang had obviously set her heart on doing
the exam so the next problem was how she was going
to write her exams with her right hand out of action.
In the end she got approval from her teachers that she
could do the exam at home.

That evening, Yuan Fang's hand was very painful.
When, however, she thought of the hopes for the
youth that the wise leader Chairman Hua entertained
and when she thought of how 'uncle' Lei Feng, had
he still been alive, would have handled the situation,
the pain disappeared. She gritted her teeth, and with
resolution in her heart and driven on by revolutionary
zeal to create socialism and overcome all difficulties,
she determined to take the exam and to do well in
order to repay the Party.

However, when Yuan Fang's mother returned
home and found out what had happened she sternly
addressed her daughter. "On no account are you to
take the exam with your hand in that state!" At this
Yuan Fang pleaded with her mother, mentioning

'uncle' Lei Feng's spirit and how he had feared no difficulties. She also brought up the need for putting the 'four modernizations' campaign into practice and the general importance of learning, as she pleaded with her mother.

"It is absolutely vital for me to discredit slogans put out by the Gang of Four that learning is worthless. Anyway, I want to be a good person. I want to be both red and expert as was Lei Feng."

Listening to this, her mother realized Yuan Fang was right, so finally gave in.

Every day from the next day, immediately after school, her classmates brought the exam papers round to her home where she did them. Her classmates and mother took turns to act as her invigilators. As she was unable to use her right hand, she tried desperately to write with her left hand so that she could fulfil the task of learning that the Party had entrusted her with. But, having never tried to right with her left hand before, she failed. She therefore dictated the answers to whichever classmate was invigilating at the time.

The biology exam, however, included the following question: 'draw a diagram of the human respiratory organs and name the parts.' Drawing with her right hand proved even more painful than writing with it. Furthermore, she found it difficult to 'speak' a diagram. This clearly put her in something of a quandary. Her mother, who was invigilating this exam, saw the position her daughter was in and advised her to skip the question. Yuan Fang, on the other hand, thought to herself,

"Workers can't turn out shoddy goods. Peasants

can't cultivate fields just any old how. Students must therefore study diligently. They must certainly not adopt a slap-happy approach to their studies."

With these thoughts echoing through her mind, she shook her head and replied to her mother, "I'm going to draw the diagram with my left hand." And, while beads of sweat bedecked her forehead, she slowly and painstakingly drew until she had produced a pretty good diagram.

On another occasion, the classmate who was invigilating her maths exam saw that Yuan Fang had made a mistake and told Yuan Fang how to correct it. Yuan Fang, however, cheerily replied,

"I mustn't change it. After all, exams are set to measure how much we have learned. And, as far as this question is concerned, well, it's enough for me that you have now told me how I should have done it.'

So she carried on for the next few days, revising in the evening and doing her exams in the afternoons. In all, she sat seven exams and did extremely well. Her revolutionary attitude of completely ignoring all hardships in the pursuit of learning was praised by everybody. Indeed, the school, in recognition of the way she had diligently studied the works of Chairman Mao, the way she had learned from Lei Feng, and for all the good works she had carried out and her study of socialist culture, named her a 'Three Good Student'.

Needless to say, she did not allow any of this to go to her head. As she herself put it,

"I must learn from 'Uncle' Lei Feng and study hard to master the concepts of socialist culture so that I can in the future become a pillar of the motherland."

She even returned to school before her hand had had a chance to heal completely. That is why it was with her left hand that she recorded the following words,

"I must strengthen my resolve. I must not let my teachers nor my classmates down. I must become a good citizen, as good as Lei Feng."

I apologize to readers for asking them to wade through this propagandist claptrap detailing the 'revolutionary fervor' of this girl who, if she had actually existed, must have been a truly poisonous human being. But it shows that Lei Feng was still being held up as a model. Stomach-churning stories, of which the Yuan Fang story is just an example, were still being published in an attempt to rouse the masses to revolutionary heights. It will be remembered that Lei Feng, the person from whom the youth of China was being urged to learn, was a sort of emasculated boy scout with a less than nimble mind. Had he actually been a boy scout in the real world, one imagines he would have remained badgeless after a futile career. He owed his chief claim to fame to a diary he wrote, called, uninspirationally, *The Diary of Lei Feng*. It is testimony to the awesome control that the Party can exert that his record of extraordinary banality and stupidity became a runaway best seller. In it, the author recounts, one assumes with pride, incidents of bewildering idiocy. Here is one such example.

One day, Lei Feng was attending a political class being given by a Political Commissar, as part of army training. He heard, as did presumably the rest of the class, sounds that he initially took to be thunder. It then dawned on him that, far from being thunder, the sounds were the sounds of shells exploding on a nearby hill. It was on realizing this that he displayed the initiative for which he became famous and revered. Assuming for reasons that are

ANDY KIRKPATRICK

never made perfectly clear that these were enemy shells—and, surely, only a brain as unfit for purpose as Lei Feng's could have assumed that these were enemy shells, given that his army unit was stationed in Central China and there was no enemy within hundreds if not thousands of miles—he proceeded to leap out of his classroom window and run off *to do battle on his own to protect the People's Republic of China.* [my italics.]

The Political Commissar felt obliged to give chase. On catching up with Lei Feng, he explained, ever so gently, that those were not enemy shells but ours. "Just a bit of target practice. Absolutely no cause for alarm."

The man's career and thus the diary, is littered with incidents like this, until his mercifully early and aptly unheroic death, which, it will be recalled, was caused by his being hit by a falling telegraph pole while he was riding in an oxcart.

This, then, was the man that the youth of China were urged to adopt as a model. It came, therefore, as a significant sign that times were changing when the students from Fudan's Physics Department put up a wall poster that asked a few questions that must have been quietly percolating in the minds of many students for many years. In essence, the wall poster asked whether the Chinese Communist Party really believed students to be of the intellectual level to be impressed by the deeds of morons such as Lei Feng. While, the question might appear trivial, this wall poster heralded a whole series of more specific ones in which members of the Fudan's Revolutionary Committee were savagely criticized and accused of crimes, including hounding people to death. One member of the Revolutionary Committee committed suicide as a result of his crimes being listed in one of these wall posters. Times were indeed changing.

24

DOWN ON THE COMMUNE LEARNING
FROM THE PEASANTS

Despite the upheavals that were taking place, we were still going on factory visits and change was also noticeable there. On the rare occasions when a 'sufferer' was not presented, it was now possible to obtain some concrete information about the factory concerned. For example, on our visit to Shanghai's No 3 Textile Factory, we learned that wages for apprentices started at 18.50 yuan a month (marginally more than the monthly stipend that students at Fudan received). This went up to twenty-three yuan after two years. The average wage at the factory was thirty-six yuan, but with the best paid receiving 112 yuan per month. We were also told that fifty percent of the nylon yarn was imported from Japan and West Germany and that fifty percent of the factory's products were exported to Malaysia and Indonesia. On our tour around the factory, one couldn't help noticing that many of the looms and other machines were standing idle, with no one manning them. When we asked about this, we were first told that this was because the factory had already fulfilled its monthly production quota. But as it was only the eighth of the month, this was hard to believe. We were then offered an alternative explanation by another official. The factory workers, he explained, had been called to another part of the factory to deal with a rush order. But when we got to the part of the factory where the rush order was supposed to be being filled, there were looms standing idle there too. We concluded that many of the workers had simply decided to take the day off. It was a hot July day and working in the heat for an average wage of only thirty-six yuan per month was not considered incentive enough. The explanations for the idle machines also reinforced how feeble the reasons given by various factory officials and spokespeople were—not just in this one—and how easily they could be jettisoned or disproved.

The Textile Factory did provide us with an unusual Gang of Four-type story, related to us during the 'short introduction' meeting. A worker had stolen some cloth. This was discovered by the factory committee. The thief's wife then somehow managed to contact supporters of the Gang of Four. They then, in the name of Wang Xiuzhen, passed judgment saying that, far from disciplining the thief, the factory committee should discipline themselves. The Gang of Four supporter who passed this judgment, Wang Xiuzhen, was one of the three who underwent mass criticism at the sports stadium, as related above. We were then told that the thief was still working at the factory and still drawing his monthly 40 yuan salary but was undergoing 're-education' after work each day. The officials did not tell us whether the factory committee had disciplined themselves.

A second factory we visited at about this time was the old British American Tobacco (BAT) company. Here the monthly wages ranged from thirty-six yuan to 130 yuan per month. The factory officials' attitudes towards smoking was interesting. The factory made cigarettes to avoid having to import them. The officials, however, were in no doubt, that smoking was detrimental to health. As one put it, "Smoking has no good points at all." He then added, and I felt probably for the benefit of the British students, "but tobacco is better than opium."

Although factory visits were now becoming more interesting as we were able to glean some real information from them, the real highlight of the Shanghai summer came when we were taken off 'to learn from the peasants'. This was the bucolic equivalent of the ten days we had spent in a factory, learning from the workers. Now, we were escorted to spend ten days on a commune a few miles outside Shanghai.

Day 1

Needless to say, the first thing we got on arrival was a meeting to give us a 'simple introduction' to the commune. The commune housed nine brigades, seventy-eight production teams, 4,600 households, a workforce of 12,000 and a total population of 20,000. Daily hours of work were from 5:00 a.m. to 7:00 a.m., then from 8:00 a.m. to 11:30 a.m. Lunch and 'rest' were from 11:00 a.m. to 2:00 p.m. Then it was back to work from 2:00 p.m. to 6:30 p.m. Fortunately, we were to be spared the crack-of-dawn 5:00 a.m. to 7:00 a.m. shift.

We were thrilled to hear that we were to be billeted with local households. I was to be billeted with the Swiss student, J — he of the Swissair catalogue. Our initial euphoria at these billeting arrangements — we were actually going to live with a Chinese family — was significantly dampened when we discovered that two members of the university bureaucracy were also to be billeted with us.

After the meeting, we were taken to our new accommodation, which turned out to be a simple but sturdy newly built two-story brick house. Two rooms upstairs — the bedrooms — and two downstairs. There was no running water or sanitation, which explained the presence of the large wooden buckets under the beds.

Our host family, a man and his wife, provided lunch, which was excellent. Beautiful fluffy white rice with no stones, gloriously fresh green leafy vegetables stir-fried with a little pork. The food was consistently excellent. Whether it was the family's typical diet was hard to say. We had each contributed ten yuan for our stay and I was unsure whether this was used to provide the meat (either pork or chicken) for our meals. Conversation with our hosts flagged a little, as there was some initial problem in understanding each other's accents. But they were friendly and did not seem at all in awe at the prospect of housing foreigners for ten days. We were able to discover that the family had built their home themselves and that it was one of a group of nine houses of the same type, each of which housed members of the same extended family.

After lunch, it was off to work in the fields. I was assigned the task of tying up row upon row of cucumber vines. After an hour or so I found this pretty back-breaking work and had to stop and stretch every so often. The locals laughed at me, but pleasantly and not mockingly, although they were keen to tell me that tying up vines was women's work. It was only then that I noticed that the only men tying up the vines were foreign students.

It was back to the house at 6:30 p.m., filthy dirty and aching for a soak in a hot bath. There were no baths, of course. The only running water was provided by a pump which was in a sort of square in the middle of the nine houses. This pump was shared by all nine houses. We joined the queue for the pump and when our turn arrived we sprayed and tipped cold water over each other and rubbed off the mud. More private areas were washed indoors with hot water poured from a kettle and using a small flannel and hand towel.

Supper was as excellent as lunch, but our hosts seemed shyer than they had been at lunch. After supper, however, the father of the family joined us as we sat outside enjoying a balmy evening. He puffed away contentedly on his pipe. We learned that they each had two days holidays a month. He said that he was very happy with his lot, and he looked it.

We were early to bed, myself hoping that I wouldn't have to use the wooden bucket during the night.

Day 2

Today we were dispatched to a different part of the commune to harvest cabbages. This was better than tying cucumber vines, but it was a big field with a hell of a lot of cabbages waiting to be harvested. After a couple of hours, the weather turned and it started pelting with rain so we were ushered into a granary where we spent the rest of the day sitting around on sacks making pieces of string out of hemp. The thundering noise of the rain on the granary roof made conversation difficult.

On returning to our house, I decided it was time to visit the outhouse. The nearest was inconveniently situated some 300 yards away. To get to it one had to walk along a narrow raised path which bisected two fields. The outhouse itself comprised two holes, side by side in the ground, surrounded by concrete walls in one of which there was an open door. The roof was made of corrugated iron. Fortunately, neither of the holes was occupied when I entered, but after a couple of minutes a local wandered in to take his place squatting on the neighboring hole. He casually popped a cigarette in his mouth, lit it, and started to smoke, while reading a newspaper. He did not address me or express the slightest surprise at coming across a foreigner in the outhouse. He did not leave with the newspaper.

After another excellent supper, during which the main topic of conversation was how best to serve potatoes so that they can be eaten easily with chopsticks, there was another meeting to attend so off we trooped. When we got there, something seemed to have gone awry with the electricity supply as the lights were giving off very little light. There was one small table in the room and several benches. The spokesman was seated at the table while we took our places on the benches. Once settled, the spokesman began to bombard us with numbers. The commune had 3,000 pigs, 300 dairy cows, 2,000 ducks and 50,000 fish. There were four 'barefoot doctors' (the evocative Chinese term given to paramedics with only very basic medical training). There was a school, there was underground irrigation for the fields, there were vacuum pumps that brought and spread human fertiliser – which explained the siting of the outhouses. The average annual income was 400 yuan, but people could farm their own plots (each forty square meters) to make extra income from selling off produce. There were several thousand trees of many varieties. Political classes were held each Friday evening.

After the meeting, I collapsed into bed, dog-tired, but with brain buzzing with numbers of trees, ducks, and pigs. I was soon asleep.

Day 3

We woke to find it was still raining but not heavily enough to prevent us from being sent back to the field to tie more cucumbers. I felt that would take me a long time to get used to this and I was soon once more reduced to an aching wreck, but this time a damp and rather miserable one. Lunch provided much needed relief. And then it was back to the cucumbers once more.

The atmosphere at meals had now relaxed and we chatted away happily and got to learn something about our host's family.

"Are the people in the nearby houses all family members?"

"Yes, one of our daughters lives next door. She recently got married. But her husband was posted to the Northeast."

'Will she be able to visit him?'

"No, no," the father of the house replied, laughing at our naivety. He will come back next year for the Spring Festival.'

This was not unusual for couples in China. They might well be posted to different work units in different parts of the country and only get to be together once a year over the annual Spring Festival holiday.

After supper we sat outside with our host drinking beer and we complimented him on the lovely food we were eating and chatted about cabbages and cucumbers. Then it was back to the meeting room, but this time to see a film, *Bitter Flowers*. Everything about the film was dreadful: the plot, the acting, the sound and the seating. Having just been drinking beer, I derived some pleasure from transposing the film's title to Flowers' Bitter, the name of a most palatable British beer. I found myself luxuriating in the thought of downing pints of the stuff.

On the way home after the film, an elderly woman— apparently a relative of our host—accosted me and fired a series of questions at me. As she was virtually toothless and speaking in a local dialect, I couldn't understand any of the questions except one, which I took to be "How much do you weigh?" Her startled reaction to my reply suggest I may have misunderstood even this question, or that I weighed a lot more than she felt I should.

Day 4

This morning we were given a change of activity. We moved from tying cucumbers to tying tomatoes. But after lunch we got a completely unexpected but most welcome break. We were taken back to Fudan to have showers, exhilaratingly hot showers! This also meant that we returned too late to the commune to work in the fields, so we were put to pickling cabbage. From this, I developed a lifelong passion for pickled cabbage.

After supper we sat outside again, again drinking beer. The after-supper drinking crowd increased day by day and some of Lyn's 'family' turned up. Given China's strict one-child policy of the time, it was eye-opening for us to discover that some families had more than one child. Our host mentioned that they had a son, so I asked whether he lived in one of the houses

"No, he lives and works in Shanghai," he replied but, more than that, he would not say.

"What do you do with your private plot?'

"We keep some rabbits and we once kept ducks on a small pond. But they all died within a year. I don't know why."

"What about vegetables?"

"Yes, of course, they'll be late this year."

"Will this reduce your income?"

"No, our income is stable."

"And how long does it take to build one of these houses?"

"Only two weeks', was the startling reply.

Out of the blue, a Spanish student suddenly announced that Spanish peasants only started to wash regularly with the advent of running water. No one seemed quite sure how to take this remark, and it was ignored.

The evening's entertainment came in the form of a rather good television film. We all crowded back into the meeting room to watch the black and white TV and a splendid thriller about evil thin moustachioed men (all male villains in Chinese films of the time were portrayed with thin moustaches) smuggling state secrets out of China to Hong Kong in remote-controlled toy cars.

Day 5
It was back to the tomatoes for the first hour and then to the dreaded cucumbers once more. But this time, we were not tying

them up, but painting the base of the plants blue. We applied some form of insecticide but I was unable to discover what sort it was. Every time I asked someone what sort of insecticide it was, they simply replied, "It's blue." This became rather trying after a while, as did the anointing in blue itself. We spent the rest of the day like this, bent over, with a little paintbrush in one hand and a pot of 'blue' in the other, daubing away at the base of the plants. Standing up straight took several minutes to accomplish.

The beer drinkers, larger in number again, gathered after supper. Tonight a prospective house builder told us it would cost him about 1,500 yuan to build his house and that the building materials were being provided by 'friends'. If this figure of 1,500 yuan was right, this would be the equivalent of nearly four years' salary.

Another film show was advertised but few of us went to watch it, preferring to sit around chatting and sipping beer.

Day 6
This was the day when we were to be taken to be shown round the commune. The day started badly for me as I noticed with pleasure that breakfast comprised dumplings, and those stuffed with pork and chives are a particular favorite. But then, after eating one I discovered it to be all dumpling and no filling. I was childishly disappointed. Then, it was off to the meeting room where members of the commune's Revolutionary Committee felt the need to reel off a whole set of numbers and figures, most of which we had been given on the first day. Some new figures were provided, however. The commune grows twenty different kinds of vegetables, has twenty cars (where are they?), 140 forty-horsepower tractors, nine paddle boats (paddle boats?) and each dairy cow gives 2,500 kilos of milk a year. There are also lots of mushrooms.

Although we had been at the commune less than a week, it was clearly noticeable that the lives and attitudes of the members of the Revolutionary Committee could hardly have been more different from those of the peasants, such as our hosts. Here were the members of the committee, sitting and lounging around the meeting room, smoking expensive filter-tipped cigarettes, noisily slurping tea. They were all well-dressed and looked smugly comfortable. My reverie was interrupted by a sudden flashing of lights and I realized I was looking at a 'you are here' kind of map, which had been propped against the far wall and a committee member was pressing buttons which illuminated where all the commune's small factories were sited.

At last, the talk was over and we actually set off to look around the commune. We saw experimental tomato plots, chickens, pigs screaming before being slaughtered, sheep and cows (Dutch apparently). We visited mushroom houses, a turnip house and a factory that made the 'human fertiliser vacuum pumps'. Then we had lunch, which was excellent and beer was served. During lunch we learned more: that the peasants can own their own homes; that they take their produce to be sold in various markets which are about four or five miles away; and that there are 700 party members on the commune. I asked a member of the Revolutionary Committee how many Party members were on the 15-member committee. Showing his training in obfuscation, he answered, "Slightly more than two thirds." I asked a second member of the committee who replied, "Eleven,"

That evening, there was a party. Back we went to the meeting room which was already full of mothers with their children and babies. The evening was grandly termed a 'concert evening'. This meant that people would pop up to perform and then we would be asked to perform. I dreaded such evenings, but it seemed there was to be no escape. I started quietly rehearsing the words of *"Ilkley Moor Ba T'at,"*

The 'concert' started with individual members of the commune standing up and reciting their own poetry to the background wail of babies. This was wonderful theater even though, or perhaps because the poetry was woeful. My attention was drawn to one member of the Revolutionary Committee spreadeagled on the room's solitary sofa. And, although the place was standing room only, there was plenty of room for a person to sit on either side of this committee member. Why did no one choose to sit next to him? I then noticed he was wearing what look to be silk socks. Being wary of committee members wearing silk socks would seem to be wise advice.

The inevitable occurred and we were asked to perform, but luckily as a group. This meant 'Ilkley Moor Ba T'at' could remain unheard, as the English group song is a polite version of 'Old Macdonald had a Farm'. For once we were a genuine hit—the children actually demanding encores as we sang and made animal noises to roars of applause, loud clapping and raucous laughter.

The Swiss pair were the last to perform. But by the time they were about to start the yodelling all Chinese expect all Swiss to be able to do, the babies took over and the yodelling was drowned out by caterwauling infants. Curtain down and home to bed.

Day 7
Another hard morning's work painting cucumbers, but a different task for the afternoon: pulling up the roots of already harvested cabbages, putting them in baskets, then dispatching them to the piggery.

The evening saw us once more in the meeting room. It was Friday night, which, down on the commune, meant it was political study night. To say people were excited about this would be an exaggeration. As the text of the evening's study was taken from Volume 5 of *Mao's Collected Works*, the lack of general enthusiasm could be forgiven. But, just as the appointed member of the Revolutionary Committee was about to explain 'What Mao meant here', he was interrupted by an elderly fellow who started to reminisce about what life was like under Chiang Kai-shek, the leader of the banned *Kuomintang* or KMT Party who had decamped to Taiwan after his defeat by Mao in the civil war. I was initially very surprised that he wasn't shut up, as not only was any mention of Chiang Kai-shek—considered by the Communist Party to be an 'arch bandit'—usually proscribed, the very fact of interrupting a political study group's task of examining a Mao text was unheard of. But, for some reason, the fellow was allowed to continue his reminiscences. One thing I remember him saying was that 150 kilos of rice or its equivalent in cash, were needed to buy off being conscripted into Chiang's army. My interest was clearly not shared by the locals. Yawns from all sides of the meeting room accompanied his tale. An elderly woman started the gentle tremble of a snore. But the old fellow's tale had the merciful result of curtailing detailed discussion of the Mao text and off we went to bed.

Day 8

We were back among the cabbage fields, but harvesting them and collecting any withered leaves for the pigs. The afternoon brought heavy rain so we reverted to the wet weather programme of sitting on grain sacks in the granary and making string out of hemp. The locals were clearly getting used to us and had become informatively chatty. There was a discussion about the fiendish complexity of work points.

"How many work points can one get in a day?"

"Usually ten. Thirteen is the maximum number but most

people actually acquire eleven or 12."

"But what about people who can't work or who are too old?"

"Old people who are not working get the equivalent of eight work points a day'

This was rather like a pension scheme, I thought.

"How are the work points allocated?"

"Every day, a comrade notes down how much work each person has done."

"And how much is a work point worth in cash terms?'

"Most people get 1.25 yuan a day."

This, if paid each day, would work out at about 450 yuan a year, more or less matching the annual 400 yuan which we had been earlier told was a typical commune member's average earnings. One of the Fudan bureaucrats chipped in to say that 1.80 yuan was the average daily 'wage' in her home village. All in all, however, it seemed impossible to find out how work points were actually calculated.

The locals then moved on to talk about the houses.

"What is the best type of house to have?"

"One of brick and with two storeys,"

"Like the ones we are living in?"

"Yes."

"Would you not prefer a typical Chinese house built round a central courtyard?"

They laughed and said I was the victim of 'old thinking'.

That night we were treated to a specialty dish for supper, 'zhong zi'. These are time-consuming to make, being made of a compound of sticky rice and flour into which pieces of vegetable and/or meat (and red bean for a sweet version) are inserted, all wrapped up in bamboo leaf and then baked or steamed. They were delicious.

Day 9

A glorious morning and we were back with the cabbages. We enjoyed this work the best, so it was with curses we greeted the news that the afternoon was to be spent tying more wretched cucumbers. The superb weather helped ease the pain, as did the knowledge that this was to be our last full day on the commune. I was sad to be leaving the commune, but delighted at the prospect of never having to tie a cucumber again. Our impending departure also made the locals talkative and they chatted once more about work points and earnings. Today I learned that men earned thirty yuan a month and women only twenty. But then I learned that, last year, a woman aged twenty-three earned more than a man aged twenty, earning an average of forty-seven yuan a month. I was becoming increasingly confused about how work points and money were distributed among the commune members. But then someone explained that all men received the basic salary 30 yuan a month but, then, at the end of the year each person's work points were totted up and any extra money earned was paid. This explained how the twenty-three-year old woman averaged forty-seven yuan a month. I then asked,

But why do women earn only twenty yuan a month when men earn thirty yuan?

"Because they earn less", was the answer.

Tonight, our final night, was to be a special night. We were even treated to a bottle of local wine with the evening meal. Our host and his wife did not drink any, but the Chinese bureaucrats did, so we finished the bottle of the rather sickly sweet red wine between four of us. I suspected we would need some Dutch courage for tonight's special party night. This turned out to be similar to the concert night, but longer, and with much more polished performances from the locals. They provided excellent live music and performed several *kuai bans*. These are a type of talking song delivered at a constant rhythm which is beaten out using wooden clappers. They can be very funny and irreverent, a living form of satire. Before long, the four English students among us were once more called upon for our rendition of "Old MacDonald", but then asked to provide an encore. I finally had to sing "On Ilkley Moor Ba T'at", with Lyn and the other two British students as my backing group. The performance was received with complete mystification. There was no clamoring for an encore. The highlight of the foreign students' performance was indubitably provided by our Spanish member's rendition of "Jailhouse Rock". This had the whole room in hysterics. Beer was drunk copiously. I went to bed pleasantly tipsy.

Day 10
Dumplings again for breakfast followed by the disheartening news that there was to be a "raise ideas" session in the meeting room at 9:30 a.m. These 'raise ideas' sessions were inevitably excruciatingly embarrassing. The thought that any ideas any of us might raise for the improvement for life at the commune/ factory/university might actually be taken seriously was, of course, laughable. If one of us did offer a critical suggestion, it was inevitably rebuffed with the standard refrain, "It is possible you do not fully understand the circumstances in our country." As a consequence, these sessions were characterized by groups of Chinese and foreigners looking silently, and often sullenly, at each other. Eventually, one of the local revolutionary committee took the floor and regurgitated the figures of the previous meetings followed by a brief speech in praise of the wonders of socialism. I started to feel an urge to thump the speaker but, fortunately, he finished before I gave into it. The session was followed by lunch and a shambolic attempt to take a group farewell photo. Our collective face was raised by the Danish student who had

thought to pen a brilliant farewell letter of thanks on behalf of us all. This went down extremely well. Then we were onto the bus to take us back to Fudan. Lyn and I both felt sad to be leaving, as I suspected did most of us. It had been a wonderful opportunity to spend a few days living and working alongside locals, all of whom had been remarkably friendly and understanding. We had all learned a great deal — and seen once more the chasm that exists between the lives of the peasants and the bureaucrats and members of the Revolutionary Committees.

25

BEIJING JUBILEE AND STUMPS AT DAYBREAK PARK

Soon after our return from the commune, the four British students started to exhibit signs of being demob happy. This was occasioned by an invitation from the British Embassy to celebrate the Queen's Silver Jubilee. The invitation entailed traveling to Beijing and spending a few days there. Further cause for celebration was that Lyn and I were to stay with our friends, the correspondent and his wife.

I was also excited for a third reason. While we had been at the Language Institute I had made firm friends with 'Basher' a third secretary from the Pakistan Embassy who had been sent to the Institute to learn Chinese. Mutual friends said that Basher and I looked extraordinarily alike -- that I was a sort of slightly whiter version. Basher and I soon found we shared a love of cricket and beer. He also had a cricket ball with him, and Basher and I amused ourselves, while driving many of the residents to distraction, by bowling the cricket ball to each other along the Institute's concrete corridors.

When Basher told me that the Pakistan Embassy had a full set of cricket equipment, we thought it would be a grand idea if we could organize some form of cricket match in Beijing once the weather allowed for it. There the idea had rested until opportunity presented itself with the celebration of the Queen's Silver Jubilee. Through brilliant organization and diplomatic cajoling, Basher had managed to persuade the Pakistan Embassy to field a team against 'Basher's All Stars', made up of the two of us plus a motley selection of New Zealanders, Irish, Sri Lankans and Australians.

The Great Day dawned and the All Stars, exuberant with anticipation, made our way to the park where the match was to be played, carrying equipment borrowed from the Pakistan Embassy and several crates of Beijing beer, which we placed in the shade under the tree which was to serve as our 'pavilion'. Having beer, we held a telling advantage over the Pakistan team as a recent directive from the new leadership in Pakistan forbad Embassy officials to drink alcohol. This directive had hit some of them pretty hard and there were a few mournful faces among their side. Their 'pavilion' tree was shading cartons of orange juice.

The match started late. First we had to get rid of footballers who were playing over the area where we were planning to play before the pitch could be marked out. Basher explained to them the importance of the occasion and of cricket in general and they ceded the ground with good grace, although bemused. One footballer among them learnt that a cricket ball is hard, as he helpfully went to hoof a stray cricket ball back to us. He limped off, looking accusingly at the little red sphere.

No sooner had the footballers dispersed than real trouble arrived. It was not easy to persuade a regimental section of the People's Liberation Army that they could not use the space they had selected for target practice, as there was a very important cricket match to be played there. And we all found it pretty hard to believe that the PLA could contemplate setting up a firing range in the middle of a public park. Anyway, Basher was not a diplomat for nothing. He buttonholed the officer in charge and went into a wonderfully painstaking explanation of why the cricket match had to go on and the PLA would have to go elsewhere. He stressed that people from many, many different countries, friends of China all, had come from all over China to play in this very special match. He said that this was the first proper cricket match to be played in Beijing, if not China, since liberation (possibly true). He went on to underline that it was the Queen of England's Silver Jubilee and that the cricket match was being played in celebration of that event (well, that was stretching it a bit). He concluded his submission by saying that the match had been organized by the people of Pakistan and that all the equipment had been shipped from Pakistan especially for the match (a grain of truth there somewhere).

There was no doubt that Basher had been eloquent and persuasive. Nevertheless, none of us could really believe it when we saw the man in charge smile, shake Basher by the hand and order his men to dismantle the targets they had set up. These had been placed so that the cricketers would have been between the guns and the targets. A sight guaranteed to concentrate the mind of any batsman is the sight of armed soldiers placing targets to one side of him who then lie down to take up firing positions on his other side.

Basher returned in triumph to our tree to announce, "The match goes on." He then went over to the Pakistan tree where he and their captain, the portly Commercial Secretary, tossed, a toss which Basher duly won. He invited the Embassy team to bat first. This was not a hard decision to make, given the worrying hollows, cracks and lumps in the wicket. I could hear in my mind a commentator saying, "This might have been an important toss to win."

My memories of the first few minutes of the match are not

so much of a stream of Pakistani Embassy batsmen walking confidently out to the middle and soon walking disconsolately back to their tree, but rather the behavior of the crowd that soon gathered to watch, what must have been to them, an extraordinary spectacle. Having no idea of cricket, they, of course, had no idea of the concept of a boundary. So, many spectators came up close to the action to watch. Again, Basher's skill as a negotiator came to the fore. His case was helped by the realization of members of the crowd that the cricket ball was extremely hard and could be hit hard and far. Although they soon retreated to some distance, many remained within the boundary and, being the helpful people they were, would gather any ball that came towards them and 'helpfully' throw it back. This rather helped us keep the Pakistan score in check. By the time we came to bat, the crowd had been well enough coached for them to understand that, in no circumstances were they to stop the ball and throw it back.

The cricket was lively. After the first two overs, it was mutually decided that fast bowling be outlawed. This was a pitch with uneven bounce. A ball that reared up and flew over a batsman's head would be followed by one that raced along the ground. Batting required a degree of concentration and a good dose of raw courage.

While the pitch proved too dangerous for fast bowling, it also proved a spinner's paradise. The batsmen's relief that they were to be spared fast bowling soon turned to desperation as they tried to play the spinners. I bowled my innocuous slow left arm's spin from one end while Basher wheeled away with his leg spin from the other. You would have thought Basher was in his element, bamboozling his embassy colleagues with the combination of his guile and the complete unpredictability of the wicket. But it must have occurred to him that this diplomatic career might not progress as smoothly as it might, if he made his Military Attaché and Commercial Secretary look like fools on the cricket pitch. Thoughts of his career saw him take himself off after three overs, having dismissed three of his embassy colleagues.

The Commercial Secretary was next to bat. As noted earlier, he was a portly gentleman of some heft, and clearly not a candidate for a quickly scampered single. This was not fully grasped by the unfortunate thirteen-year old son of the Second Secretary whom the Commercial Secretary had joined at the wicket. Keen to keep the run rate ticking over, the young boy called for a quick run and set off up the wicket. There was a panic-stricken cry of "No" from his partner, but this the boy either didn't hear or chose to ignore. In any event, by the time he had reached safety at the other end, the Commercial Secretary had only managed to waddle a couple of yards down the wicket before being comprehensively run out, without facing a ball. Fuming with anger, he returned to the Pakistan tree. I did wonder how the Second Secretary's diplomatic career might be influenced by his son's eagerness for quick singles.

When the Pakistani innings folded, they had scored 126. Between innings, orange juice and Beijing beer were taken under the separate trees. And then it was the turn of the All Stars to bat. The lower order batsmen, Basher and I included, felt confident that we wouldn't be required, so possibly imbibed more beer than we sensibly might. Our confidence was based on the knowledge that one of our opening batsman was a New Zealander who had played first-grade cricket back home. We also had a gun Sri Lankan batsman and a couple of Australians who had decent cricket pedigrees.

So we lower order batsmen were sitting companionably under our tree with beer bottles in hand as we watched our two openers go out to bat. We had hardly had time for a sip before the New Zealander was on his way back, having been bowled first ball. He had made the crucial mistake of trying to play correctly. He had foolishly presented an impeccably straight bat to the first ball and been bowled, remarkably, as the ball shot along the ground under his bat to hit the wicket. "A bloody long way to come for one ball" someone rather unkindly observed. It soon became apparent that the only way to win would be to adopt the unorthodox and try to hit each ball out of the park. Once the three batsmen in our side who really could bat were out, we had a chance. The cross-batted sloggers went in and followed this tactic: leg down the wicket, huge heave across the line. We made the runs in quick time and ended up winning by six wickets. A famous victory for Basher's All Starts in what was, I believe, indeed the first game of 'proper' cricket played in Beijing since 1949.

The game was followed by post-match celebrations. At one stage we found ourselves at the hotel where the Pakistani airline crew were billeted during their stop overs. This meant the hotel could put on an excellent curry that we enjoyed that evening. After the meal, a group of us, well sprung with wine, as PG Wodehouse might say, were chewing the fat and setting the world to rights. One of our number, the journalist with whom Lyn and I were staying, started to expound a complex economic theory. While he was talking he was waving a large bottle of Beijing beer in his right hand, using it to emphasis certain points. His marginally incoherent argument was hard to follow, but I noticed that Basher was moving his head along with the waving beer bottle as if hypnotised by it. He then suddenly moved forward, removed the beer bottle from the speaker's hand, and drained it in one fluid movement. 'I must, in future, remember to cut down on the hand gestures' muttered the journalist.

The rest of the evening remains a blur. I do remember having a drink with the Finnish student who had become the janitor at his Embassy as a way of extending his time in China, and a large Icelander who was, I later learned, found asleep the following morning at the entrance of a Beijing factory.

The next few days were taken up with parties of one sort or another, punctuated by periods of deep sleep in comfortable beds and occasional sight-seeing. There was a party at the British Embassy to celebrate the Silver Jubilee itself. On being introduced to the Ambassador, a Chinese student who had recently returned from his studies in England, announced "I'm only here for the beer." This was the tag line of a popular beer advert back in the UK. The student endeared himself to me as, without knowing it, it had delivered a remark of savage irony. For, even on Silver Jubilee Day, the embassy booze was as strictly rationed, just as it had been for our welcome party last year when I had been discovered by the Ambassador himself in the embassy kitchens in pursuit of more beer.

There was a trip to the Ming tombs with one of the more hedonistic of the Beijing press corps. Far from treating the visit as a cultural outing, he plied us with Bloody Marys and then set up the empty cans of tomato juice on stones and popped away at them with the air rifle he had also brought with him.

Throughout Silver Jubilee week we had had a great time, behaved less than well on occasion, and felt just about revived enough to face with equanimity our return trip to Shanghai and our final few weeks at Fudan.

26

DENG XIAOPING RETURNS

I returned to Fudan to find myself at the center of a minor controversy. I had written another article for the *Far Eastern Economic Review*, which had this time been translated into Chinese by someone from the Fudan bureaucracy. It had then been the subject of a political discussion meeting attended by the Fudan bureaucracy and selected students. My roommates had both been at the meeting. Significantly, they said that they had actually agreed with some of what I had written but not all of it, but also explicitly said that, publicly, they would espouse the conclusion handed down by the bureaucracy that I was a 'counter revolutionary element'. We then had a long discussion about the article. The article itself was of no consequence. That my roommates were prepared to talk to me about it and tell me it had been the subject of a political discussion was. It might seem strange, but it was a sign that more practical and liberal factions were winning the power struggle. The key question at this time – June 1977 – was whether Deng Xiaoping was going to make or be allowed to make a political comeback. The general feeling was one of optimism and that Deng's return was only a matter of time. One of my roommates went as far as to say that Deng would return "very fast".

The Modern Chinese Literature course was also showing signs of revivification. Authors who had been, literally, unmentionable a few months earlier, were resurfacing again, being mentioned in lectures for the first time in years. I have already recounted Ba Jin's miraculous renaissance from the tomb. Chinese students taking the course were now being asked to write essays (in itself remarkable as the students had never formerly been required to write anything) about these newly revived authors. This, naturally, they found extremely difficult to do as many knew nothing about the authors concerned, as they had been proscribed. But suddenly, proscription became prescription.

If, however, any of us had entertained thoughts that this gentle slide towards liberalism would alter the behaviors of the bureaucracy, we were soon disillusioned. Such thoughts were mocked as being 'wild and false dreams'. Certainly, personal letters from overseas were still being opened and read, and still as amateurishly as ever. For example, one letter had taken forty days to arrive from Belgium. When it eventually arrived the recipient was surprised to find that the Flemish in which the letter had been written had been translated into French by the censors (presumably they were short of Flemish speakers), but they had neglected to rub out the French translation. Inside, however, was a little message of the type airlines insert into luggage to say that it had been searched, which read "The Communist Party Leads in All Things." When the student complained that her letter had clearly been opened, the Fudan bureaucracy inventively blamed it all on 'Taiwanese saboteurs'. On another occasion, one foreign student received a letter in which two pages from a letter intended for another student had mysteriously been inserted. Letters in which photographs had been included routinely arrived missing the photographs. We used this to irritate the bureaucracy in our personal letters home where we might say we were enclosing three photographs but deliberately only enclose one or two in the hope that the censors might be frantically searching for the missing photos. To such childish antics were we reduced by an authoritarian but frequently inept bureaucracy.

It was also during this hoped for period of liberalization that, one Sunday afternoon, I was hauled before the bureaucracy and asked where Lyn and I had spent the previous Saturday night. We had spent that night in the flat of expatriate friends who worked for the Chartered Bank in Shanghai. It was very odd that I should be charged with this at this stage as we had spent the occasional night away with them and also occasionally with the equally gracious Hong Kong and Shanghai Bank couple. I knew that the bureaucracy would have known about this for months but they had turned a blind eye. Now, however, I was told that Lyn and I would not be allowed to sleep off campus (and thus together) again. Those two bank couples may not have realized it, but they helped to keep a third couple sane and smiling.

It seemed as though those in power knew that their time was limited so that they increased their level of nasty bloody-mindedness. On July 7, two Swiss students had been chatting to an old chap by a bus stop just outside a local noodle shop. But as the old man turned to board the bus he had been waiting for, he was grabbed by a third person and marched into the nearby bus ticket office. The Swiss followed him in, but when they got there, there was no sign of him or his kidnapper

Other evidence of the unease felt by those currently in power was the appearance of official wall posters. The Security Police started to put up a rash of posters warning people against assuming that a new order was on the horizon. These posters warned people of 'illegal black markets'. One such poster announced that 'to make something and sell it was illegal', suggesting that many people were now doing just that.

Local markets started to spring up, but these were tolerated, not least because there was a serious food shortage at the time. Meat was rationed. The university was close to running out of food. The noodle shop had no meat to sell with its noodles. Standard fare became noodles with pickled vegetables. But there was still beer. Fortunately, I loved noodles cooked in this way. Noodles with pickled vegetables and beer remains one of my favorite meals today.

With the absence of the usual pork and chicken, butchers started to display and sell different types of meat. One local butcher filled his window with rows of dogs' haunches hanging off hooks, with the dogs' heads displayed in trays beneath them. Dog head soup made a nourishing broth.

For the man in the street, the general mood was a combination of happy expectation tinged with anxiety that those currently in power would somehow manage to retain it. There was also the fear of reprisals. Who knew whom might be targeted when it came time to settle the accounts?

However, there was no doubt that there was more of a spring in the step of the local students as they wandered around the campus. There was a giddy feeling that things were actually changing for the better. Deng represented hope for the future. The Gang of Four had been a bad dream. Curiously, Hua Guofeng himself was not rated highly. As part of the justification process establishing Hua's assumption of the Chairmanship, it was put about that Mao had said to him, on his death bed, "With you in charge, I'll rest easy." Most people found it very hard to believe that Mao had anointed Hua in this way. This claim on the part of the Hua faction was treated with a cellar of salt by most people. I was, nevertheless, startled to overhear one Chinese student loudly announce in the canteen that he thought his brother could do a better job than Hua. But then, I did not know who his brother was.

The July days passed with the Chinese waiting expectantly for the announcement of Deng's reinstatement. Lyn and I were also expectantly ticking off the days, but for a different reason, as we were due to leave Fudan in August. Then, on July 22, and a day after similar posters had been displayed in Beijing, posters went up in Shanghai to say that Deng had been reinstated to the positions of power that he had previously held. The news was officially confirmed in a radio broadcast on that day. People had hoped that either Hua or Deng himself, or both, would speak but neither did. However, the constant repeating of the broadcast allayed fears and people started to believe.

There followed two days of controlled celebration. There was a huge rally in central Shanghai that no one appeared to be able to get to. Lyn and I ended up jammed in a huge crowd in one of the streets leading to the square where the rally was purportedly being held and saw nothing of the rally itself. We were in good company.

Fudan had a go at laying on celebrations but the university faced a serious problem. It had been designated as the Shanghai headquarters of the Gang of Four and many senior administrators and members of the Revolutionary Committee owed their positions to Gang of Four patronage. Several had already been criticized. Anticipating the settling of accounts, one member of the Revolutionary Committee had committed suicide; others were to follow. This was hardly the atmosphere for a party.

Fortunately, Lyn and I were able to celebrate in more traditional fashion. We had a few drinks. In my case, a few too many. We had gone, that evening, to meet a friend from Beijing who had come to stay in Shanghai for a couple of days. He had nobly arrived bearing two bottles of scotch and we sat and drank whisky in his hotel room. Sensibly, Lyn knew when she had had enough and took herself off to cycle back to the university. Insensibly, after consuming the best part of a bottle of very fine scotch, I left in the early hours to cycle home. I must have managed to mount my bicycle because I remember arriving at the hump-back bridge that crosses the Soochow Creek. I also remember that I could see that the hump of the bridge might present something of a challenge. As it so proved. Each time I tried to accelerate to get enough speed to get over the hump, I wobbled and fell off. On about my fourth attempt and as I parted company once more with the bicycle, the bicycle chain fell off. There I was, lying on my back on the upslope of the bridge underneath a bicycle. This suddenly seemed to me incredibly funny and I burst out into hysterical laughter, with tears streaming down my cheeks. So, in the early hours of a Shanghai morning, I found myself lying on my back underneath a bike on a hump-back bridge giggling hysterically. Just then a bicycle transporting a Chinese version of the Good Samaritan hove into view. On seeing me lying prone under my bike, he dismounted and walked across to ask if I was all right. His question set me off into a further bout of inane giggling. This did not put off this saintly chap, however. He gently levered the bike off me and wordlessly replaced the chain. He then asked me where I was supposed to be going. I must have been able to answer this more or less intelligibly, for he helped me up on my bike and then rode alongside me with one hand on my handle bars to ensure I stayed on board. And thus did he escort me back to the main gate of Fudan, a distance of some five miles. When we arrived, he took his hand off my handlebars, whereupon, I fell off once more and burst into more laughter. He now smiled and rode off into the early dawn.

Almost immediately, the night porter turned up to see who was laughing so raucously outside his gate. I was able to persuade him I was a bone fide student and he opened the gate to allow me to wheel wobblingly to bed.

27

FINAL EXAMS

The change in atmosphere had, as noted earlier, led to one development that was not universally welcomed by the local students. This was the new ruling that they would now have to submit essays and that these would be marked. Until then the local students, most of whom came from the 'correct' class background of being a member of worker, peasant or solider families, had been able to sail though their university studies without being examined or having to pass exams. Being 'red', and thus a loyal supporter of the CCP, was considered far more important than being 'expert', or actually knowing anything about the subject one was supposed to be studying.

The foreign students, on the other hand, did have to submit an assignment and pass it in order to graduate. Those of us doing literature would receive a Graduate Diploma in Modern Chinese Literature on successful completion of our assignment. The assignment we were set was not arduous. We had to submit an extended essay or mini-thesis of some 10,000 Chinese characters on a relevant topic. We could choose the topic but it had to be okayed by the lecturers in charge. Astonishingly, given the efforts the bureaucracy had made to keep us apart, Lyn and I were told we could submit a joint assignment. It would never have occurred to us to even request such an arrangement, but we happily accepted the offer. As we were not interested in writing about the CCP's chief propagandist, Guo Moruo nor in critiquing Mao's poetry, that left writing something about Lu Xun as the safest bet. As we had visited his home town we decided on the topic of 'The effect of his hometown on Lu Xun's short stories'. This topic was duly approved.

We worked on our assignment—it was actually an enjoyable and rewarding exercise—and duly and proudly handed in our ten thousand-character assignment by the due date. We were then told that the assignment would not be examined by the Fudan lecturers but would be sent, along with the other foreign students' assignments, to the Ministry of Education in Beijing to be examined. We were also told that it was not possible to tell us when we might hear whether we had passed or not.

A nervous wait then ensued. We had no idea what the implications might be were we to fail the assignment. Might we be forced, like the poor Sudanese student, to repeat and only allowed to leave China when we had passed?

After about a month, the assignments were returned. Lyn and I received a 'good' mark but, at the same time asked to revise our assignment. The examiner pointed out that we had made insufficient reference to the works of Mao in our assignment. We were therefore required to re-submit it, ensuring that it was peppered with references to Mao. This we did. We simply identified Mao quotes that could conceivably be considered relevant and then sprinkled them throughout the paper. We re-submitted our assignment. Two weeks later, back it came, with the 'good' mark now confirmed.

This was a good lesson learned. When I came to be assessing the essays of Chinese students at Australian universities, I was able to let them know it was not necessary to justify their arguments by citing from Mao and, if they did, they would have to reference these citations, as Australian readers could not be expected to possess an in-depth knowledge of the works of Mao. I also tried to get across that they did not need to justify their position or argument by referring to Mao—or to some sage of the Confucian past—but that they could argue for alternative positions.

A second lesson learned while studying at Fudan was the value of having classes in academic literacy alongside the literature and politics classes. We had actually asked for these to help us make sense of some of the lectures and, to its credit, Fudan provided us with a weekly class taught by a lecturer who actually taught aspects of academic literacy rather than political propaganda. In my later life at Australian universities, I always stressed the importance of providing classes in the relevant disciplinary academic literacy alongside content classes; and that these should be for all students not just international students for whom English was not the first language.

On the occasion of our first lesson in Chinese academic literacy, the lecturer noticed that I was writing with my left hand. He quietly approached me and, still without saying anything, he gently tried to remove the pen from the left hand and transfer it to my right. I naturally resisted, saying,

"But I'm left handed."

"But you should always write with your right hand", he replied, "It is impossible to write Chinese properly with your left hand."

In this he had a point, but only if one is using a writing brush and writing Chinese calligraphy. The sweep of the brush in a left-handed person results in characters that look slightly odd, as the strokes are 'painted' in a different direction from those written by a right hander. In any event, I remained left-handed.

28

Departure and an altercation at the China Travel Service

Lyn and I were able to smile happily along with others at the news of Deng's return and not solely because we were happy at having passed our assignment and to be leaving China soon. We figured that anyone had to be better for China's future than the Gang of Four. Hua, who was now Deputy Chairman of the CCP and Premier, was always only going to be a makeshift short-lived Chairman, and, as earlier noted, was not considered a viable leadership material by most Chinese. We felt some sympathy for Hua as he had managed to maneuver China through what was virtually a civil war and get rid of the Gang of Four. But Deng's rise was inexorable and he was able to get his plans for economic reforms passed in the late 1970s, when he became the de-facto leader.

Things were definitely changing and for the better, but not quite soon enough. As soon as we had the precious exit visas stamped in our passports, Lyn and I set off for the Shanghai branch of the China Travel Service to organize our trip to Hong Kong. China had relaxed some of the restrictions for where foreigners could visit and Hangzhou was now 'open'. So we asked the man from CTS for tickets to Canton, stopping for a few days in Hangzhou on the way. The face of the man from CTS suddenly somehow assumed a hangdog looked. He drew a large intake of breath that made a sucking sound against his gap-filled teeth, looked towards the ceiling and announced the time-honored phrase of non-cooperation.

"There could be a problem," he murmured

"What problem?"

"The Canton train does not stop in Hangzhou"

This might well have been a problem had it been true. But, having dealt with Chinese bureaucracy for some time by this stage, I tried a different tack.

"Well, we'll take the train to Hangzhou. Get off, spend a few days there and then get the train from Hangzhou to Canton."

A few further seconds of silence, further sucking of teeth. Again he looked heavenwards.

"There could be a problem."

"What problem?"

"The first-class seats on the Hangzhou train are fully booked. There are no seats."

"Good. We want second-class seats anyway."

Another pause for silence except for the sound of his intake of breath whistling over his teeth.

"There are no second-class seats on the train to Hangzhou."

It was at this stage that several months of built-up frustration in dealing with the Chinese bureaucracy came pouring out onto this one man. I reached across the counter grabbed him by the front of his jacket, jerked him towards me and unleashed a torrent of abuse. They say that such behavior makes you lose face in front of the Chinese. All I know is that we got our second-class train tickets to Hangzhou. The man from CTS had the final word however. As we were leaving, he shouted at me,

"Your attitude should be better. Never forget you are traveling in the People's Republic of China!"

As if one could. And then, in a shout to Lyn,

"You should not marry a foreigner."

Fortunately, Lyn restrained me from turning back to beat the crap out of the guy.

The one sad aspect about leaving Fudan was saying farewell to our roommates. Lyn had shared with a jovial tubby girl of peasant stock who knew absolutely nothing about Chinese literature. Her other roommate was a girl who had been a member of a dance troupe and had traveled widely. She had even spent some time in Tibet with the dance troupe. But when we eagerly asked her questions about Tibet, she was unable to answer any of them. In typical Chinese fashion, the dance troupe had been completely self-sufficient, to the extent of taking their own cooks and provisions with them, even their own tents, so they would not have to stay in Tibetan hotels or hostels. We were amazed to find out that she had never tried any Tibetan food or drink. In her turn, she was amazed that we were amazed.

"Why eat anything else when you can eat Chinese food?" she asked.

A numbingly parochial view, but one shared by many of her compatriots. She also extended this view to matters of race and was perplexed how Lyn could marry 'outside the race'. But, despite these 'Central Kingdom' attitudes, she got on well with Lyn and tears were shed on parting.

Lyn's roommates had bought her a sensible leaving present, one that could be easily packed. My roommates, on the other hand, decided that I should not forget them for one moment on our journey to Hong Kong. They gave me a large landscape painting, but not in the form of an easily-rolled scroll. The painting came complete with an ornate gilt frame. I could just manage to get it under one arm in order to carry it (This actually takes second-place in the unsuitable leaving present stakes. On leaving the Philippines a few years earlier, my host gave me a carved teak door stop which stood two-foot high and weighed ten kilos. This might not have been so bad had he not given it to me at the airport after I had checked in my luggage.)

My roommates and I had got on pretty well despite occasional arguments about the meaning of life. Unlike Lyn's roommates, mine were both well-educated and well-connected. One was the son of a PLA general and the other the son of Shanghai cadres. When I returned to Shanghai a couple of years later, the changes running through China made it possible for me to track the Shanghai roommate down. Not only that, I was able to breeze in, unannounced and go straight to his office, which was in the Ministry of Health. It was an extremely emotional and cathartic meeting. He sobbed while apologising for the bad treatment that had been meted out to foreign students. He explained that he and Xiao Men, my other roommate, had had no choice but to spy on me and report what I said to the university authorities. Through his tears, he said how distraught he had felt at not being allowed to make friends with me or any of the other foreign students. We hugged and I found myself also shaking with sobs.

The Canton train duly stopped in Hangzhou. We were met at the station by the ubiquitous CTS. I had some concerns that the Hangzhou representative might have heard about my behavior in Shanghai, but, if he had, he gave no indication of it. In fact, much to our surprise and delight he informed us that we were free to explore Hangzhou at our leisure and on our own. Here was further evidence of significant change. This was the first time we would be allowed to be tourists without a guide to watch over us and to make sure we visited only CCP-approved sites.

We took ourselves off and booked into the grand Hangzhou Hotel overlooking the beautiful West Lake, one of China's most painted beauty spots and one celebrated in verse by countless poets. We walked slowly round the lake. It was difficult to believe we were in the same country as the one we had left only earlier that day. Lovers walked hand in hand and canoodled on lakeside benches. Fruit juice sellers were doing a brisk trade. Fat carp were gliding in abundance under small stone bridges. It was a gloriously peaceful scene and the tranquility of the lake seemed to wash away some of the pent up frustrations of living in Shanghai. A few glasses of chilled Hangzhou beer helped.

On our return to the hotel, I dismantled my parting gift and left the frame by the waste paper basket.

On the second day we went out to see the Buddhist caves but found them relatively difficult to view as the light was poor. It was just about possible to make out the many carved Buddhas in their niches for which the caves are known. After groping our way through the caves, passing several loving couples, also groping but in a different sense, we returned to town and next found ourselves in an antique shop looking longingly at a pair of paper thin six -inch high porcelain jars. Looking longingly as they were priced at 600 yuan, the equivalent of five months of our scholarship. Also looking longingly, as it was a beautifully laid out shop, full of exquisite items of jade and porcelain. It certainly provided a stark contrast to the last antique shop we had been in in Shanghai. That had been stocked with European' left-behinds'. These included a porcelain figure of a bikini-clad maiden lounging by the seaside and a cone-shaped glass container of Elizabeth Arden nail polish. This could be had for three yuan.

As we walked out of the cool seclusion of the antique shop, we were soon confronted with day to day reality. First an elderly beggar approached, withered hand extended. Then a girl who can't have been more than eight and wearing a ragamuffin dress came up and suddenly lifted up her dress to expose thighs and tummy covered in red sores.

On our return to the hotel, we were told that there was a message for us. A message? Who could this possibly be from? We had not factored in the long arm of Fudan bureaucracy. The message informed us that we owed the Fudan library seven yuan for overdue books, seven yuan that remains owed.

The next day provided us with one of the best days of our time in China. The weather was perfect. Blue skies, just a hint of a breeze. We took the bus to the famous Dragon Well tea plantation and spent the day wandering through the plantation, over hills, through small woods, following streams with crystal clear waters and coming across beautifully designed open-plan tea houses where one could sip tea and, when hungry, eat. This was our first experience of a China that the poets had immortalized in verse. I could imagine the great Li Po sitting across the table at one of the tea houses, downing cups of wine while discoursing on the vagaries of life.

After this perfect day, we went back to the hotel, packed and headed off to the station to catch the Canton train. The dismantled frame was still by the room's waste paper basket. We climbed aboard and spent a few hopeful minutes thinking we might have the six-bunk 'hard-sleeping' section to ourselves. But then I heard my name being called. I looked out of the window to see a panting bellhop from our hotel carrying the dismantled picture frame. Unluckily he had seen me so I had to go to the door of the train. 'You forgot this!' he cried, gleeful that he had managed to return the wretched frame, and thrust it into my hands. This time, I left it on the train.

Our hopes that we might be alone in our six-bunk section were soon dashed. Much panting and wheezing announced the arrival of a very fat lady from Hong Kong and her three equally fat children. They all slobbered, reminding me of a family of overweight bulldogs. And the middle child was also a screamer – and he screamed throughout the night, calling for water. His younger brother spent most of the time with one arm outstretched in my direction and making machine-gun noises with an imaginary gun. There were times when I wished it was real. The mother and the eldest child, a daughter, simply stared at me with vacant expressions for what seemed like hours on end.

We were extraordinarily grateful, therefore, when the train pulled in to Canton station. But not so grateful to see, waiting for us on the platform, a representative of CTS. We soon discovered he was of the Shanghai rather than Hangzhou CTS school. He presented us with two tickets for Hong Kong and a bill for thirty yuan. As the tickets cost only 3.70 yuan each I felt justified in asking what the extra yuan or so was for.

"Taxi to hotel now. Taxi from hotel to station tomorrow,"

I knew the hotel was about half a mile from the station but, as this was to be our last day in China, I determined not to get into any arguments with Chinese bureaucracy and to try and keep smiling through to Hong Kong. As it was we spent a pleasant enough day. We took a bus to the top of White Cloud Mountain from where the view gave a sense of space and calm, but the calm was interrupted by loudspeakers sited at the top of the mountain which blared the usual CCP guff. It was then we realized that one of the reasons why Hangzhou had seemed so peaceful was that there were no loudspeakers. It had been such a joy to walk around the lake and tea plantations listening to nature and not to propaganda being blared at you.

The restaurant where we had lunch – mercifully not the same one where we had eaten a year earlier on our entry into China – was full of people from Hong Kong who appeared to be entertaining their Mainland relatives. Money and class divide was in evidence. The Hong Kongers were smoking Winston cigarettes and the younger ones wearing blue jeans. A portly Hong Kong businessman was being trishawed slowly towards the restaurant, while the old man riding the trishaw strained and grimaced.

The following morning, it was time to get the train from Canton to 'freedom' and Hong Kong. Surprisingly we found ourselves sharing a compartment with the Hong Kong football team. We must have seemed rude as we gawped at their fashionable clothes and customized haircuts. Then we were at the border and customs. This was nerve-wracking. Had we done anything to prevent us from leaving? Would they let us out? Symptoms of China paranoia syndrome. In the event, both sets of border officials were polite and courteous and we were soon back on a train and on our way to Kowloon. The first thing we noticed were the cars. Beijing and Shanghai had been cities of bicycles. Only top cadres traveled by the black ominous-looking Red Flag limousines. Then it was how polite people were (something that the Hong Kong Chinese themselves found difficult to believe). First stop off the train was to a pub, the White Stag. All those wonderfully colored bottles arrayed on the shelves. Being able to talk to the barman without worrying that he might be led away and questioned by the security police. The barman's mother, on hearing us chatting to her son coming out of the kitchen. She telling us, in an unmistakeable Shanghai accent, that she was originally from Shanghai and asking us, "Have you been there?"

29

FRIENDSHIPS IN THE FRIENDSHIP STORE

This all happened more than fifty years ago. The title of this book, The Friendship Store, seemed an appropriate, if slightly ironic, title for describing what life was like in China at the time. Although the few foreigners that were in China were officially referred to as 'foreign friends', they were not allowed to get close enough to Chinese to be able to make friends. Any Chinese who approached a foreigner to strike up a conversation, or if only just to say 'hello', would run the risk of being whisked off by a member of the seemingly ever-present security police.

The bureaucracy and the CCP combined to make my day-to-day life difficult, while officially heralding the everlasting friendship between China and the peoples of the world. It had been a difficult time and Lyn and I were glad to 'escape' into Hong Kong. When I arrived in China I was excited about being able to enter a country whose culture I had studied for several years. I had dreams about becoming a translator of contemporary Chinese novels. But a few months of the Modern Chinese Literature course at Fudan soon had me deliberately shunning almost all of the 'literature' that we were allowed to read. It was mostly CCP propaganda dressed up as novels of socialist realism.

When I complained about the brain-deadening diet of the Modern Chinese Literature course to J, the Swiss student, who was one of the few taking the Classical Chinese course, he simply said,

"Why waste your time reading that modern rubbish? Read something like this instead."

So saying he thrust into my hands a copy of Liu Xie's *The Literary Mind and the Carving of Dragon (Wenxin Diaolong)*, a book of literary criticism written in the 5th Century.

It would be stretching the truth to say that I immediately became hooked on classical and medieval Chinese. But the fact that such texts were not off limits to foreign students and were available from the Fudan library meant they could be borrowed. Since leaving China, I have focused on the study of the history of Chinese rhetoric. The proscriptions around the reading of modern Chinese literature had a happy result in that they opened the door to the treasures of classical Chinese.

My experiences of living in China put me off all things to do with Mainland China for at least two years. When I was interviewed for a job with the Star, a tabloid newspaper in Hong Kong, I let the editor, an Australian, know that I had been in China. Immediately on hearing this he roared, "I don't want any of that Commie crap in this newspaper."

"There is little danger of that," I replied. Thus reassured, the editor promptly hired me.

After two years in Hong Kong, China was less and less anathema. At the same time, life in China under Deng Xiaoping was becoming less restrictive. Lyn and I decided to return as tourists and visit places that had been off limits. It was on this trip that I met one of my roommates, Zhang, at his office in the Ministry of Health in Shanghai. And it was at this meeting in his office that he broke down in tears while apologising for spying on me. I was soon also reduced to tears as we hugged each other.

Despite the best efforts of the Chinese bureaucracy, deep respect and genuine friendship between Chinese and 'foreigners' could be nurtured.

During this visit, my enthusiasm for things Chinese started to return. Since that 1979 visit I have returned several times. For example, I spent a semester in the early 1990s at Beijing University as part of my doctoral study into Chinese Rhetoric, which I undertook while studying at the Australian National University in Canberra. I have twice been a visiting Professor at the Beijing University of Astronautics and Aeronautics. I have attended numerous conferences. Over the years, I have made lifelong friends with many Chinese. The 'Friendship Store' has actually been able to create long-lasting friendships between foreigners and Chinese, despite all the obstacles and restrictions.

Since the 1970s, there have, of course, been almost unbelievable transitions in many walks of life. While the Beijing and Shanghai of the 1970s were cities of bicycles, today there are seven ring roads circling Beijing, a city of constant traffic jams. While Shenzhen was a small border village, now it is part of a huge conurbation with a population of 13 million. This extraordinary development was in large part the result of Shenzhen being named the first Special Economic Zone (SEZ) by Deng Xiaoping in 1980. Similar developments and change can be seen across China. China has the longest high speed rail network in the world. You can now get from Hong Kong to Beijing by train in around nine hours. It took me more than thirty hours when I did the journey in 1976. The first manned Chinese space flight was in 2003.

The changes have not been confined to infrastructure. The level of literacy has risen dramatically. Almost all Chinese can read Chinese today. Only around twenty percent of the population was literate when the CCP assumed power in 1949.

Workers today would be able to read the works of Mao at political study sessions in their factories. The material well-being of the people has also increased in extraordinary ways. Those 'before the revolution/after the revolution' speeches that I recount in the book would sound very impressive today. The current GDP per capita is around $12,500 compared with virtually zero in 1970. As for poverty levels, a recent World Bank report has noted that China has lifted 800 million people out of poverty. So, it has to be said, that the CCP has done an incredible job of improving the material quality of its people's lives.

Until recently, there had also been a shift away from the importance of being 'red', along with the recognition that China needed experts in order to develop. The resurrection of Deng Xiaoping in 1978 was an early sign that experts might be replacing ideologues and propagandists.

"It doesn't matter if a cat is black or white, as long as it catches mice," as Deng famously said.

Post-Deng, the presidencies of both Jiang Zemin (1993-2003) and Hu Jintao (2003-2013) also saw a slight loosening of CCP control. For example, academics started to take over the running of the universities, replacing the previously all powerful Communist Party functionaries. I was able to teach my own curriculum during the semesters I spent as a visiting professor, without interference. But in recent years, this has changed to some extent, and I have recently turned down invitations to teach in China as a result.

So, has China returned to the political climate of the 1970s? Friendships between foreigners and Chinese have always had to take into account the role of the CCP. Who in the classroom or the staffroom is the CCP stooge or informer? But it was much easier to make such friendships in the first two decades of this century. Now, it seems that some of the practices of the 1970s are returning.

But, even as I write this, I can see a photograph of a recent doctoral student of mine, standing with her husband in Shenzhen, while she is beaming and proudly holding their recently born daughter. And on my desk is a photo of me with one of my greatest Chinese friends along with two academics, both of them my doctoral students and who are now among my closest friends.

What of the future? Are there lessons for China's current leaders to draw from the turmoil of the 1970s? Maybe there are. Noted scholar Wang Yuhua, in an essay on what the CCP can learn from Chinese Emperors, pointed out that choosing a loyal and competent successor is extremely important. Those emperors who chose such a successor, were sixty-four per cent less likely to be overthrown than those who did not. Emperors who designated a loyal and competent successor lived longer.

Mao was clearly aware of these lessons and, in 1966, did designate a successor, Lin Biao, whom he thought to be loyal and competent. However, the relationship between them soured and Lin Biao died in an air crash in 1971, while flying over Mongolia. Details of the crash remain obscure. Was he fleeing because he was about to be purged by the CCP? Was Mao in any way involved? In any event, he was classified as a counter-revolutionary traitor after his death.

After this, Mao failed to nominate a successor until, as I recount in the book, on his death bed, he is said to have nominated Hua Guofeng with the words, "With you in charge, I'll rest easy."

The lack of a designated successor between the death of Lin Biao in 1971 and Mao's own in 1976 provided fertile ground for competing cliques to try and seize power from a clearly ailing and mentally deteriorating Mao. In this civil war-like period, the Gang of Four was paramount, creating the repressive conditions described in the book.

The arrest of the Gang of Four allowed the resurrection of Deng Xiaoping. In time, Deng designated Jiang Zemin as his successor, which allowed for the peaceful transfer of power. Jiang Zemin also designated his successor, Hu Jintao and, once again, in 2012 there was a smooth handover of power. Hu Jintao nominated Xi Jinping as his successor in 2012, a move tinged with irony given the way he was unceremoniously ushered out of the closing ceremony of the Party Congress in October 2022. Deng established an informal limit of two five-year terms for the party leader, an arrangement that was abandoned at that meeting. But perhaps the leaders today could consider dynastic history and the aftermath of Mao's death. Otherwise, history suggests there could be consequences. My hope is that China will be able to return to the trajectory of growing transparency and diversity, and greater integration into the world that overall marked the Deng era. But for now, in some ways, it seems 'The Friendship Store' is returning to the 1970s.

About The Author

Andy Kirkpatrick was born near Liverpool but grew up in what was then Malaya and Singapore, being sent to boarding school in England from the age of 7. Growing up in Southeast Asia instilled in him an interest in the cultures and languages of the region. After obtaining his degree in Chinese Studies from Leeds University, he was a postgraduate student in Beijing and then Shanghai from 1976-77. He then worked as a journalist and language teacher in Hong Kong before returning to the UK to study for an MA in Linguistics. He has worked in tertiary institutions in the UK, Hong Kong, Singapore, Myanmar, China and Australia, where he received his PhD in Chinese rhetoric from the Australian National University. He is Emeritus Professor at Griffith University, Australia, and a Fellow of the Australian Academy of Humanities. He divides his time between Bern, Switzerland and Reigate, England.

Milton Keynes UK
Ingram Content Group UK Ltd.
UKHW040652111124
451038UK00009B/155